# Wings Over the Pacific

THE SEVENTH AIR FORCE IN WWII

*A History in Photographs*

# Wings Over the Pacific

## THE SEVENTH AIR FORCE IN WWII

*A History in Photographs*

STEWART FERN & LEE FERN

Commonwealth Book Company

ST. MARTIN, OHIO

First published in 1947 by Stewart E. Fern.
New Edition © 2017 by Commonwealth Book Company
All Rights Reserved

ISBN: 978-0-9905351-8-8

## YOU OWE...

YOU MEN of the 7th Air Force and allied organizations who find this book in some measure an answer to your requests for a pictorial record of your days in the Pacific owe your thanks to the documentary and combat photographers and AAF public relations teams who kept their cameras trained on combat and ground crews from island to island, on falling bombs at target after target. Without the bulldogged perseverance of Major Hulbert Burroughs and his documentary photographers there would be no consistent picture library upon which the editors have generously drawn. To public relations men such as Lt. Col. Dickson Jay Hartwell and Major Lynn Poole goes credit for seeing the scope of pictorial coverage for the folks at home. To Fred Noer of the Indianapolis Engraving Company you owe thanks for on-the-job interest beyond the call of an engraver's duty. For months of laborious and monotonous pouring over lists of the 7th's veterans and mailing of announcements, please share my thanks to Lee Fern, my co-editor and wife.

Stewart Fern.

TO THE MEN OF THE SEVENTH AIR FORCE WHO WILL NEVER COME HOME THIS BOOK IS DEDICATED IN RESPECTFUL AND HUMBLE GRATITUDE

# JAP FLAG AAF VERSION

**FLIGHT FROM HAWAII** to Tokyo might be divided into twelve periods, targets or campaigns designated by this AAF version of the Jap Empire's rising-sun flag. The 7th's fighters and bombers, joined by the '29's, skip-hopped into the Jap homeland 45 months after the Empire's fleet had bombed Pearl Harbor—to set the sun!

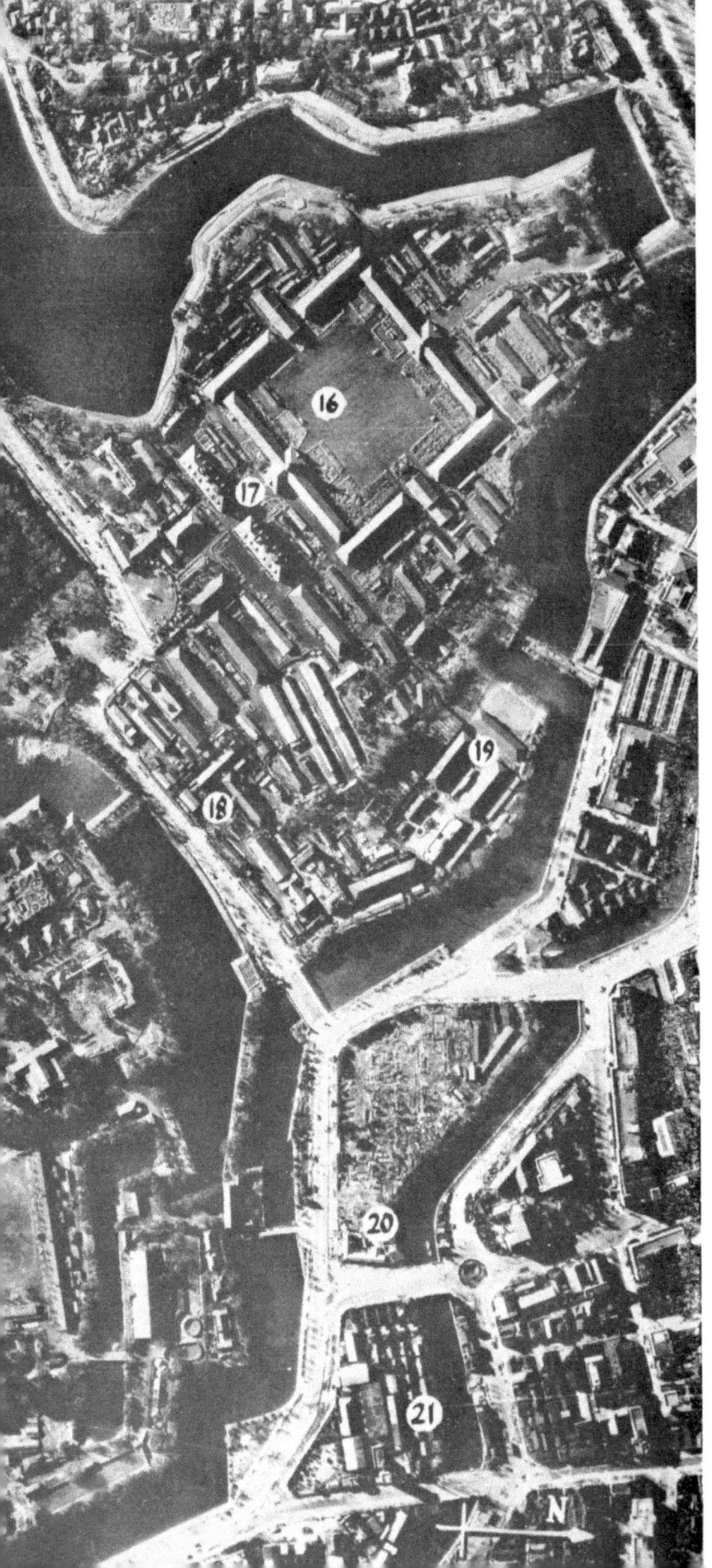

# END OF THE LINE!

**WHEN THE BOMBERS** and fighters of the 7th left Hawaii to begin blasting bases across the Pacific, this was the last stop, the final objective—the palace of the Emperor of Japan in the heart of Tokyo.

As each new striking base was won the Ellice-Gilbert, Marshall-Mariana-Ryukyu march, the men of the 7th subtracted so many more miles to go to this ultimate Pacific target.

The remarkable photograph was taken by the giant lenses in the cameras of the famous photo reconnaissance B-29, "Yokohama Yoyo", at about seven miles up.

Spiritual center of a spiritually militaristic nation, the area here shown is honeycombed with defenses of the once-imperial person of Hirohito.

The concentration of Japan's historical and national symbols in this photo is evident in the legend below.

(1) Imperial Palace (2) Dep't. of Imperial Household (3) Parade Grounds (4) Statue of Kusunoki (5) Twin Bridge (6) Seimon—Main Gate (7) Sakurada Gate — Where Treaty with Perry was signed (8) Dep't. of Justice (9) Police Hq. (10) Metropolitan Fire Dep't., Training Center of Police Dep't. (11) (12) Momiji Mountain (13) Imperial Gardens (14) Anti-Aircraft (15) Kudan Hospital (16) Imperial Guards (17) Hq. B'ld'g. (18) Inspecorate General of Military Education (19) Hq., Army Fortifications Dep't. (20) Central Meteorological Observatory (21) Ministry of Education (22) Palace Police Dep't. (23) Chiyoda Archives (24) Cabinet B'ld'gs. (25) Privy Council (26) Anti-Aircraft (27) Anti-Aircraft.

# HAWAII

**THIS IS WHERE THINGS BEGAN** for the Seventh. Training, supplies, recreation, staging... From here West, it was all "forward area".

# SHIPBOARD
### ALL THE JOYS OF A CUNARD CRUISE !!!

# ELLICE ISLANDS

First Damned Islands Before the Others . . .

# GILBERTS

MAKIN, TARAWA—THIS IS WHERE WE BEGAN TO DISH IT OUT . . . .

TARAWA

# MAKIN

16

# BAKER ISLAND
### INTERLUDE

**BAKER** was a haymaker in reserve. Few in our own forces knew we were there. No Jap did.

**ERNIE PYLE,** bless his soul, never heard of Kwajalein. A lot of Joes who moved in to take it wished they hadn't. The 7th's men staging interminable raids on Truk could have done without it.

Beer Bust . . .
Coral Dust . .

Likker Lust... Women Fust... THAT'S # KWAJALEIN

# KWAJALEIN

# "SAIPAN IS A LOVELY GARDEN ISLAND..."

**A FEMALE WAR CORRESPONDENT** said the boys wanted to return here to homestead. Just ask Corporal Taylor, page opposite!

25

# GUAM

**HEAVY WITH** head quarters, Guam wa where you tried to sta out of someone's hai and vice versa. Bu steamy and jungled it wasn't half bad fo sweating out a war.

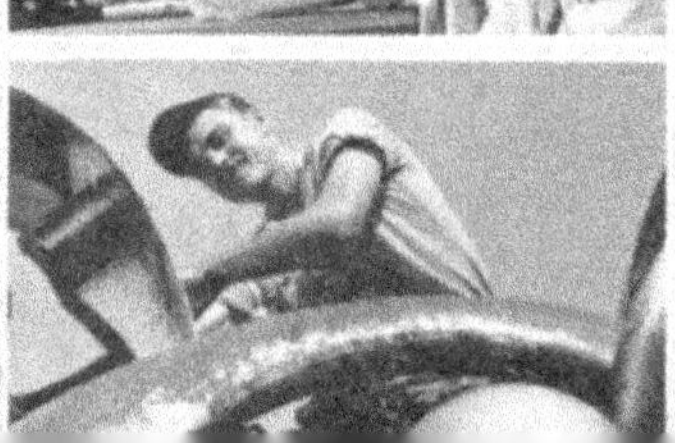

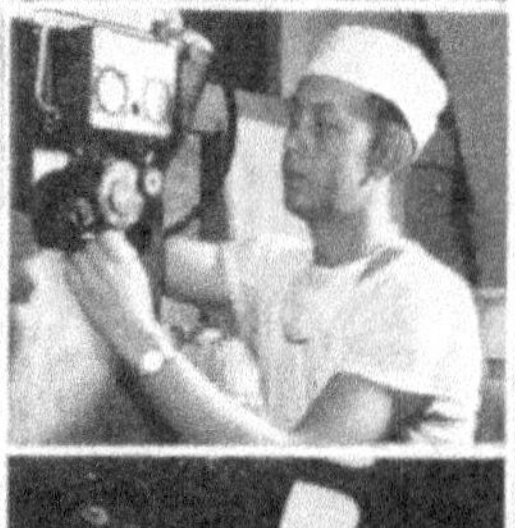

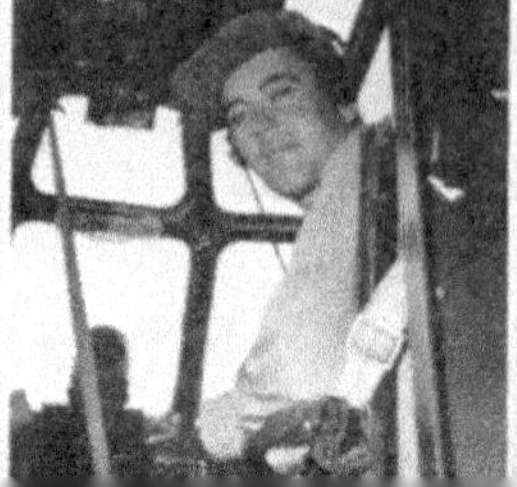

GUAM

# ANGAUR

**THE 494TH DUG IN HERE EARLY,** carried the Seventh's fight all the way to Corregidor.

# WITH THE HEAVIES

# I W O J I M A

This was the cin[der]
heap halfway [to]
Tokyo from [the]
B-29 bases of [the]
Marianas. This [is]
where the M[us]-
tangs swarmed [up]
to escort the b[ig]
tailed birds o[ver]
the Empire capit[al.]
Only the Mari[nes]
who took the ro[ck]
and the AAF pil[ots]
who tried to fly [off]
it knew what I[wo]
really was. T[he]
burned out cities [of]
the Jap capital [at]-
test to its sign[ifi]-
cance.

# IWO JIMA

# OKINAWA

**FINAL WAR BASE OF THE SEVENTH,** Okinawa was on the Jap's front porch. Fighters and bombers were geared for a ceaseless and merciless raking of the Empire homeland when the Nips tossed in the towel.

# OKINAWA

34

**AFTER THE CORAL ATOLLS,** the men of the Seventh thought they had come home when they set up first camps under the pine trees of Ie's temperate zone. Kamikazes shortened the sensation.

# IE SHIMA

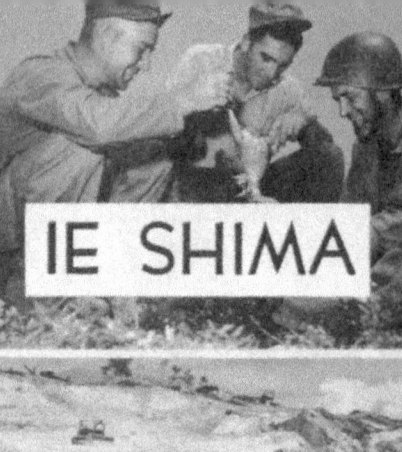

# IE SHIMA

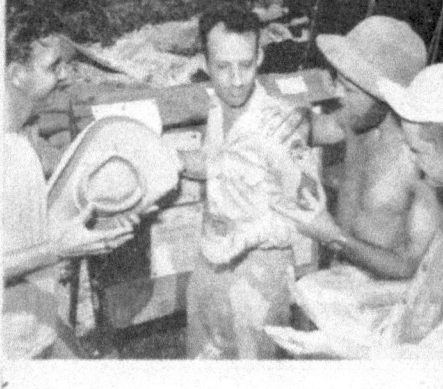

36

# BLACK WIDOW

**FROM A PADDLEFOOT'S** foxhole on Saipan, a yellow burst in a black sky was a comfortable sight. A P-61 had not only intercepted, but eliminated, another Jap.

# P47

**WHEN A GENERAL** visiting Iwo Jima said, "Where the hell are the 47s?" he was thinking of the Thunderbolt's incomparable record. The flyboys of the 318th can tell a few stories from the Saipan log.

# LIBERATORS

# B 24

B 24 became a symbol . . . the personality of the Seventh.

**THE JAPS** on every target island from Tarawa to Iwo Jima came to know the Liberators better than their Zeros. To them, the

B-24

43

# P 51

**WHEN THESE WAS**
swarmed in at l[ow]
level for the first re[con]
of the enemy ma[in]
land, it was really [a]
terrific party. A[ll]
the Superfort cre[ws]
intimated they lik[ed]
having the little bu[g]gers around duri[ng]
the bomb runs o[ver]
Tokyo. Like a terr[ier]
with a Saint Berna[rd,]
it made a great tea[m]

P-51

45

# B25

**CANNON-PACKING, ROCKET-WALLOPING,** gun-toting bombers, the Mitchells made a mess of the Marshalls. They were downright nasty at Nauru. Peace stopped the picnic they began from Okinawa.

# PHOTO RECON

**UNARMED WITH ANYTHING** but speed, the P38F5s of the 28th PR laid out the targets and assayed the damage for the Seventh on the march across the Pacific.

# TARGETS

HAHA JIMA

# BY-PASSED MARSHALLS

TRUK CANCELLED

TRUK, MIGHTY JAP BASTION HAS BEEN CANCELLED OUT. 7TH AAF BOMBS DESTROY THE ENEMY'S FLANKING THREAT TO AMERICA'S PACIFIC DRIVE.

**TRUK**

GOVERNMENT BLDGS

TANK FARM

PORT FACILITIE[S]

BEFORE

52

OIL DOCK

**TRUK**

TOWN WIPED OUT

TANK FARM

**AFTER**

# TARGETS

**TOP**, Saipan in foreground, Tinian beyond, as seen from a pre-invasion mission; left center, frag bombs rip up Iwo's beaches in the softening campaign; right center, a pillar of smoke marks the end of an enemy strongpoint on an island off Ponape in the much-bombed Carolines; below, a broad view of Yap, bombed and by-passed.

# TARGETS

**TOP LEFT,** Marcus under regular bombing to keep it from any flanking threat; top right, Wake took plenty from the early days of the Seventh's march until the end; lower left, bomb of a B-25 skips over a Jap ship; but most didn't; lower right, Japuti Island at Ponape gives a typical view familiar to Pacific bombardiers.

CHICHI-JIMA

# THE BONINS

# BASE BUILDERS

# AVIATION ENGINEERS

**WHEN A LIBERATOR PILOT** on Saipan said, "Those are the babies that are winning the Pacific war", he was pointing at a bulldozer, not a B-24.

# ENGINEERS

**WHEN ANYBODY** had a dirty hauling job, he just called in the . . . .

# TROOP CARRIER

# FLIGHT NURSE

**THEY WEREN'T ANGELS** but they wore wings, and they looked good to a guy who needed help in a hurry.

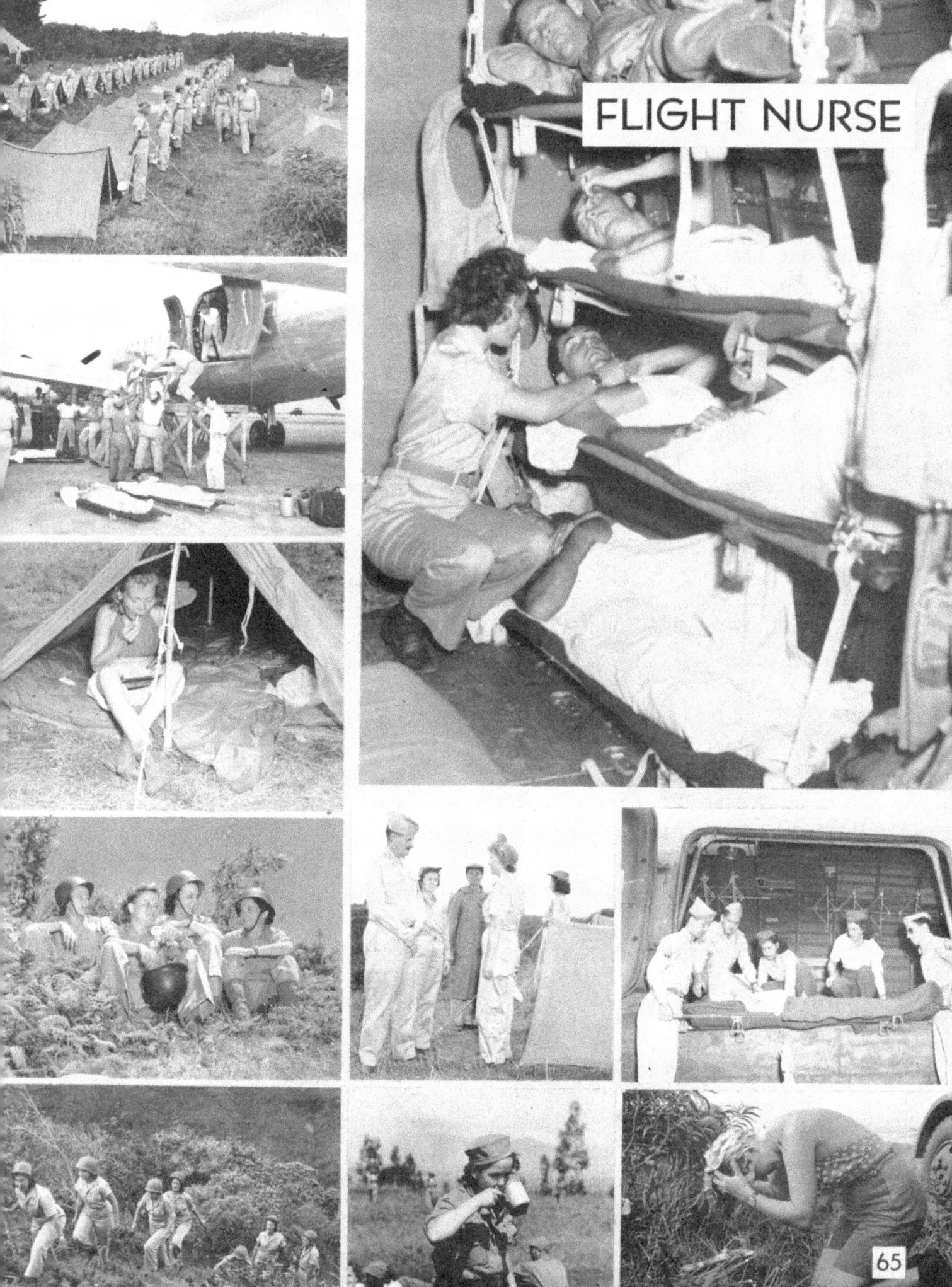

# GRASSHOPPERS
L-5s of the 163rd.

# FOXHOLE FAITH

**A MAN'S RELIGION** was pretty basic in a bomber, 500 miles of water from base

# SERVICE SANS SMILE

**A G.I. SELDOM** took himself seriously, but he maintained a growling sort of grimness in the performance of his job.

# NIGHT JOB

**AIRSTRIP CONSTRUCTION, NIGHT MISSIONS,** 100-hour checks, C.A.P. or just C.Q. . . . the graveyard shift wasn't a homefront invention.

# WASH WASH WASH WASH

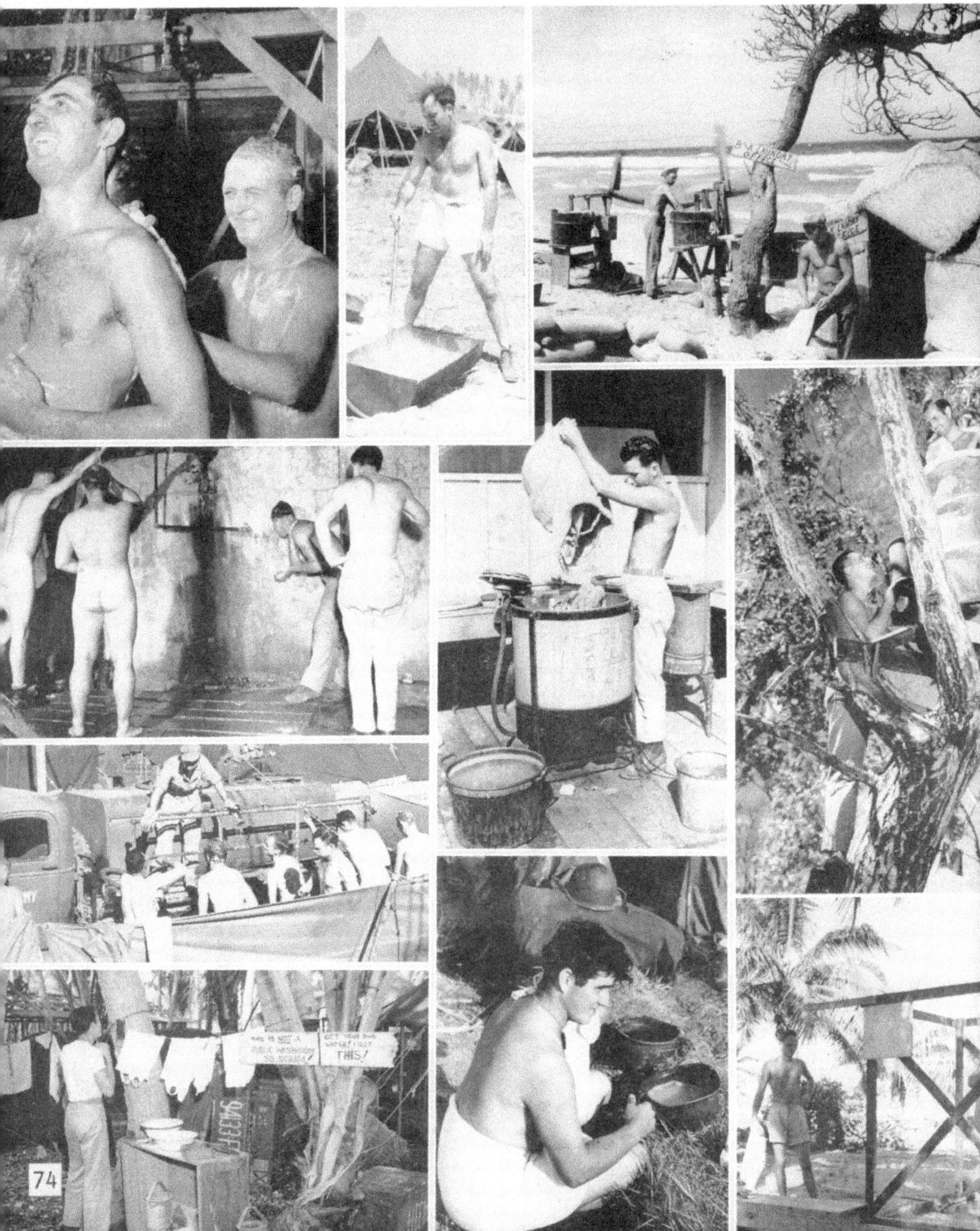

# WASH WASH WASH

Your ears, your feet, your messgear or your shorts... "Who does your laundry?" had but one reply on a coral atoll.

When the Seventh left Oahu  
The diet was terrific;  
The tin can list was booed and hissed  
As spam became prolific.

As corned beef hash and carrot cubes  
And fruit drink made with powder  
Were dished up fifty thousand times  
The hue and cry grew louder.

For a dozen isles, a thousand miles,  
We camouflaged or spiked it.  
Now home again, we beg for steak,  
But eat canned spam and like it!

# AT LEAST 8,756,495,687,417,666,202

# 875,649 CANS OF C-RATIONS

# BUT YOU MEET A LOT OF PEOPLE

NATIVES

# M.O.S.

# JOBS

82

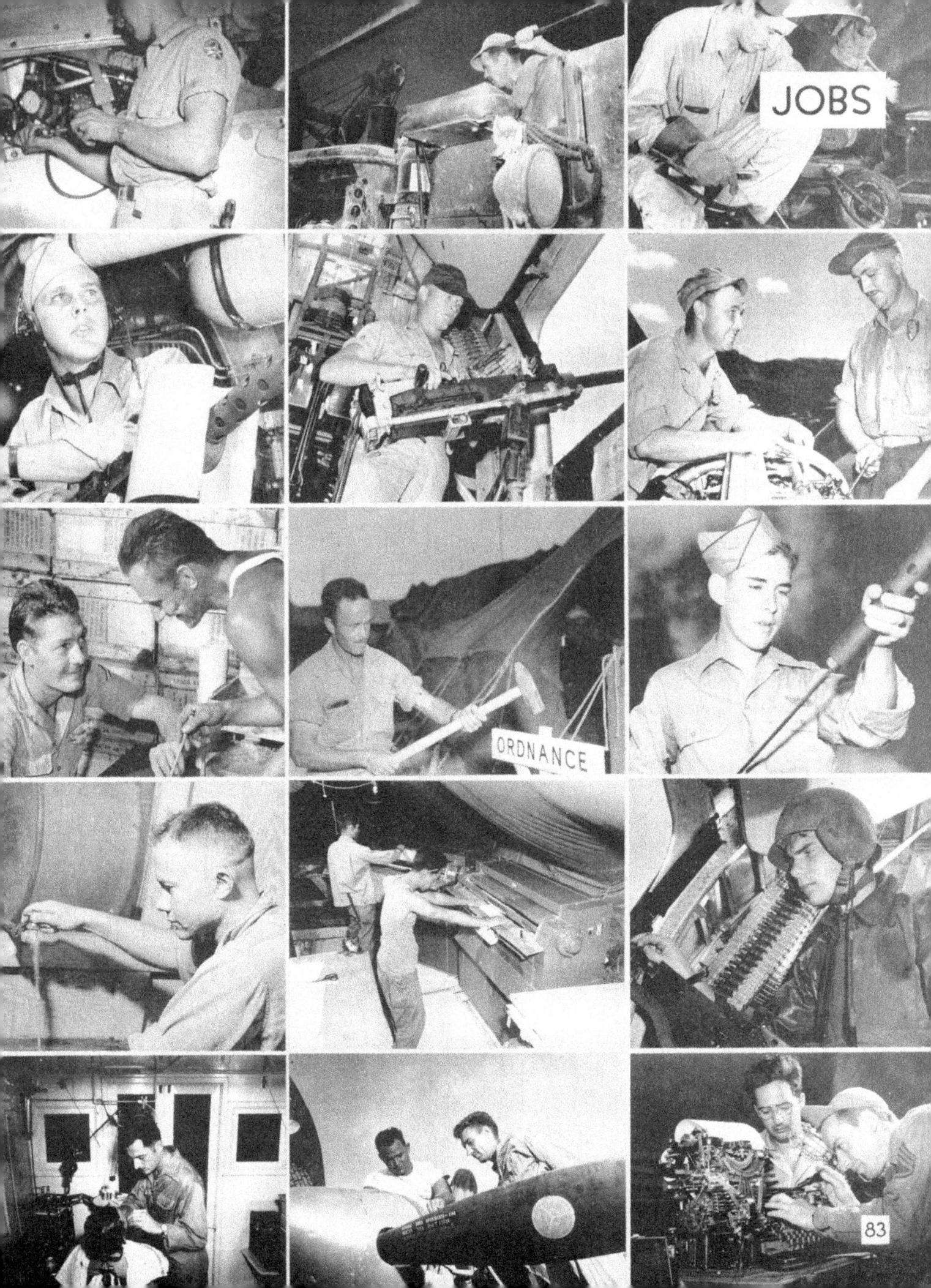

JOBS

ORDNANCE

JOBS

**WHEN YOU WEREN'T WORKING,** eating or sleeping, what to do on a stamp-size atoll presented a problem. **BUT IT'S WORSE WHEN YOU'RE ON YOUR OWN**

# RECREATION

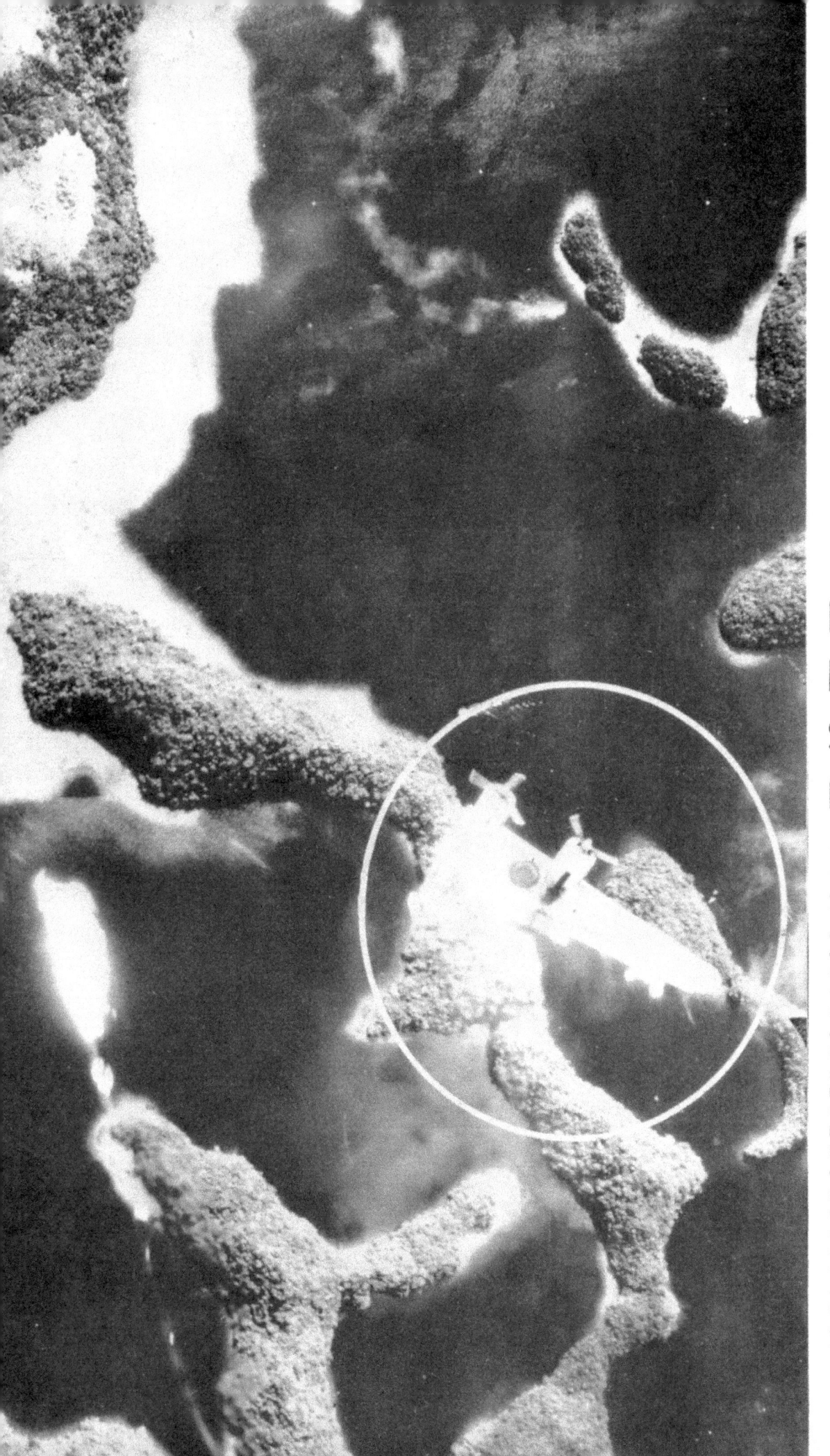

# BY-PASSED ISLAND STRIKES BACK...

In the Spring of 1945 over the by-passed enemy island of Koror in the Palaus this 7th AF Liberator which was making the bomb run with other B-24s of the 494th Bomb Group (see clusters of falling bombs at arrows) was hit squarely by a heavy anti-aircraft shell which blew off its left wing. Engines are still turning on the dismembered section (see circle). Flipped on its back, the big Liberator's open bombbays had not yet released the load of 500-pounders. As the plane crashed in the heavy growth, one of the 11-man crew was seen to parachute. He was listed as missing. Regularly striking by-passed Jap islands, the 7th Air Force Liberators kept Japs neutralized as other forces worked closer to Japan.

RECREATION

# GRASP AND GRIN — Shake Hands With The General, Son!

# EXPRESSIONS?
## PIPE THESE PANS!

**ON THESE PAGES** are just a few of the hundreds in the Seventh who earned and got a medal and an official HQ handshake.

# HQ.

# HEADQUARTERS

95

# BRASS

**WHEN YOU SAID "THE OLD MAN"** in the Seventh Air Force, you meant age in skill and savvy. AAF CO's and CG's were usually one of the boys—just pilots who had flown a little longer and knew a little more.

BRASS

# HQ. BOMBERS

BOMBERS

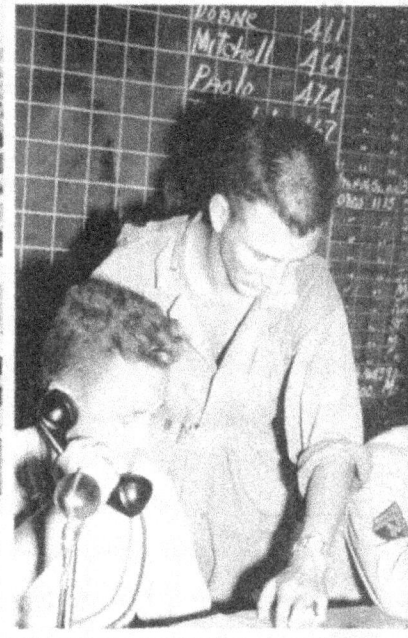

# BOMBERS

# HQ. FIGHTERS

# FIGHTERS

103

# AND THEN THE BIG-TAILED BIRDS WERE EVERYWHERE

When the B-24 crews on Saipan saw the aviation engineers building 8000-foot airstrips, they knew that, after their half dozen island hops from Hawaii, they were now to take a second place in the Pacific air war.

The arrival of the first Boeing giants was sweated from day to day. At Isley field and the first one over brought a hearty cheer as it mimicked the agile pitchout of welcoming P-47s. From the start, the Bee TwoNines were in solid with the Seventh.

By the time the Thanksgiving Day news of the Superforts' raid had reached the world, the pattern of parked giants had covered Saipan's south peninsula. The Liberators moved down a notch to Isley number two but kept up the hammering of Iwo's hidden army.

Not many men of the Seventh—fighter or bomber or groundcrewman, will forget the sight of a B-29 rendezvous high over the island as one after another of the big-tailed birds dropped off the runway and gained speed over Magicienne Bay.

# HQ. SERVICE

HQ. SERVICE

# R.S.V.P.

**IT NEVER WAS** a one-way war, for the Japs knew how to fight back. From Funafuti to Okinawa, it was smart to know how to duck. Iwo counter-banzais, noontime attacks by Zekes on Saipan, suicide landings at Oki made a helmet and a carbine standard operating equipment for a Tokyo-bound airforceman.

# R.S.V.P.

# DIRECTORY

Editor's Note: We have made an effort to list in these columns the names of the men as they appear in this book. Addresses have been brought up to date where we have been able to maintain contact with the men. Some of the Seventh's members here listed are dead. But we have listed them, as we have included their pictures in this book, because we believed their families and friends would want to see their names and faces among the men who helped make the Seventh the biggest little air force in the world. A great many of the men appearing in "Wings Over The Pacific" do not know they have been so recorded for we had insufficient record of their addresses. If you should let them know, we're sure they would appreciate it.

| NAME | ADDRESS | PAGE |
|---|---|---|
| **A** | | |
| Abraham, John | 3333 N. Marshfield, Chicago, Ill. | 25 |
| Abramson, Maurice | 812 Raleigh, Glendale, Calif. | 90 |
| Acre, John P. | Fay, Okla. | 101 |
| Adams, Chester F. | 622 S. 5th, Clinton, Ind. | 92 |
| Adams, Orland P. | Rt. 1, Palestine, Ark. | 66 |
| Adams, Wayne | Guthrie, Minn. | 90 |
| Adams, Woodrow R. | Warren, Ark. | 101 |
| Adler, Jerry | 2121 Whitley, Hollywood, Calif. | 91 |
| Agee, John F. | 2943 Sixth, Forth Worth, Tex. | 85 |
| Alexander, Louis | 1154 Hancock, Bridgeport, Conn. | 20 |
| Alexander, Sidney J. | | 63 |
| Alford, Julius E. | 125 Audubon, Montgomery, Ala. | 37 |
| Allen, Carnell | | 95 |
| Allen, Hargus | | 12 |
| Allen, John | 9 Whiting, Lowell, Mass. | 20 |
| Alshouse, R. H. | Orlando, Fla. | 29 |
| Alter, Adrian | 5945 Vickery, Dallas, Tex. | 60 |
| Alvey, Charles H. | 719 E. 4th, Casper, Wyo. | 26 |
| Anderson, Glenn L. | 314 W. 12th, Sioux Falls, S. D. | 102 |
| Anderson, Harold J. | 316 Fourth, Eau Claire, Wis. | 82 |
| Anderson, Jesse B. | Batesville, Miss. | 77 |
| Anderson, Truman F. | 616 E. Knox, Galesburg, Ill. | 102 |
| Andresen, Harold W. | 210 Sparks, Sioux City, Iowa | 66 |
| Andrews, Richard D. | | 63 |
| Andrich, William M. | 14418 Lappin, Detroit, Mich. | 36 |
| Apana, Irvan | Box 142, Wiamanalo, Homestead, Oahu, TH | 83 |
| Armstrong, Hugh W. | 910 W. Airline, Gastonia, N. C. | 62 |
| Anold, H. H. | | 96 |
| Arp, Floyd | | 63 |
| Artz, Fred R. | 18945 Roselawn, Detroit, Mich. | 92 |
| Ascough, Howard M., Jr. | 114 W. Mt. Pleasant, Philadelphia, Pa. | 24 |
| Ashenbrenner, Robt. L. | 2012 S. 7th, Missoula, Mont. | 92 |
| Atkinson, S. W. | Pacli, Ind. | 46 |
| Attison, Sam | 809 E. Strong, Pensacola, Fla. | 24 |
| Augusta, John J. | 269 Clark, Auburn, N. Y. | 70 |
| Austin, Vance L. | Franklin, Minn. | 24 |
| Austin, Waldo E. | | 63 |
| Ayres, Frank L. | 631 Clarence, Lake Charles, La. | 102 |
| **B** | | |
| Bachner, Ambrose W. | 125 Burr, Pittsburgh, Pa. | 24 |
| Bailey, Elmer J. | Box 164, Uleta, Fla. | 92 |
| Bailey, O. E. | Box 91, Maple Rapids, Mich. | 11 |
| Baines, Melvin L. | 4325 Idaho, Houston, Tex. | 82 |
| Baird, Donald H. | Rt. 5, Box 292, Bakersfield, Calif. | 103 |
| Baker, Douglas S. | Skipperville, Ala. | 85 |
| Baker, Harold H. | Rt. 1, St. Joe, Ind. | 61 |
| Baker, John W. | 920 York, Cincinnati, Ohio | 90 |
| Baldwin, Ned H. | 3011 Bay-to-Bay, Tampa, Fla. | 90 |
| Balester, Frank P. | 4044 Lillibridge, Detroit, Mich. | 102 |
| Balkum, Everett L. | 111 Belmont, Jackson, Tenn. | 25 |
| Balmer, Glenn G. | 3525 Decatur, Denver, Colo. | 25 |
| Balogh, Joseph C. | | 63 |
| Bancum, B. C. | Oxnard, Calif. | 61 |
| Barchek, Michael E. | 115 Overbaugh, St. Clairsville, Ohio | 20 |
| Barfield, Marvin D. | | 63 |
| Barker, Coy | | 95 |
| Barner, William A. | 310 Birch, Rt. 7, Spokane, Wash. | 66 |
| Barnes, Joe L. | 502 E. Jeff, Clinton, Mo. | 46 |
| Barnes, Wendell W. | Tulsa, Okla. | 93 |
| Barnhill, Eubanks | Rt. 3, Tallahassee, Fla. | 93 |
| Barnsley, Robert L. | Ozone, Ark. | 24 |
| Bartley, John A. | 16 Sherman, New Rochelle, N. Y. | 24 |
| Bartlett, Richard | 3705-64th, Woodside, L. I., N. Y. | 24 |
| Barton, Elmer F. | West Roxbury, Mass. | 33 and 34 |
| Bashori, Christie F. | Middle Point, Ohio | 85 |
| Basore, Robert R. | 1725 NW 34th, Oklahoma City, Okla. | 37 |
| Basterfield, William | Lorain, Ohio | 29 |
| Bates, James M. | 120 River, Davenport, Iowa | 95 |
| Bathauer, Raymond | 543 Lower, Kohler, Wis. | 11 |
| Bearden, Bennie P. | Decatur, Tex. | 48 |
| Beatty, Richard A. | 209-28th SE, Charleston, W. Va. | 92 |
| Beaulieu, Lucin A. | 610 Rimmon, Manchester, N. H. | 77 |
| Beck, Henry T. W. | 1845 W. Mulberry, Baltimore, Md. | 34 |

| NAME | ADDRESS | PAGE |
|---|---|---|
| Becker, Roy | Fairbanks, Alaska | 33 |
| Beckerleg, Ernest E. | 158 Lucas, Grass Valley, Calif. | 92 |
| Beckwith, James O., Jr. | 48 Grove, Burlington, Vt. | 97, 101, 102, 103 |
| Beddall, Joseph | Jerome, Idaho | 46 |
| Bedell, David P. | 134 N. 3rd, Duquesne, Pa. | 33 |
| Bedingfield, Talmadge | 205 N. Brevard, Charlotte, N. C. | 76 |
| Bedwell, Floyd H. | Fresno, Calif. | 87 |
| Belesi, Anthony A. | 564 Grand, S. San Francisco, Calif. | 68 |
| Bellinger, Dean S. | 3716 31st Pl, NE, Washington, D. C. | 21 |
| Bemis, William | 150 Agard, Auburn, Calif. | 21 |
| Bennett, Horace D., Jr. | 705 Fifth, Williamsport, Pa. | 62 |
| Beresford, Tom | Gen Del, Boston, Mass. | 85 |
| Berg, Carl A. | Criple Creek Mining Co., Folger, Alaska | 33 |
| Bergeric, Peter | 2 E. Crawford, McKeesport, Pa. | 27 |
| Berheim, William A. | 4325 A Essex, Emeryville, Calif. | 21 |
| Bernet, Marian | 3221 E. Mont, Dormant, Pa. | 11 |
| Besche, Victor O. | Baltimore, Md. | 25 |
| Bestoso, Edmond J. | 148 W. Division, Holbrook, Mass. | 66 |
| Betesh, Al | 6824 Bay Pkwy., Brooklyn, N. Y. | 34 |
| Bevington, Jack | 354 N. Adams, Akron, Ohio | 61 |
| Bialosky, Joseph | 1248 Cedar, Cleveland, Ohio | 29 |
| Bican, David S. | 4615 Jewett, Cleveland, Ohio | 83 |
| Bice, Clarence L. | 1501 Larch, Raymond, Wash. | 21 |
| Bigelow, Ray C. | 1102 Robeson, Fall River, Mass. | 84 |
| Billingsley, Jack F. | 18 Fulton, Newark, N. J. | 25 |
| Bindas, George J. | 1806 Oakwood, Youngstown, Ohio | 32 |
| Biondi, Carmine | 1260-55th, Brooklyn, N. Y. | 24 |
| Bishop, John A. | 101415 Crocuslawn, Detroit, Mich. | 24 |
| Bishop, Russell A. | 229 Elm, Northampton, Mass. | 84 |
| Black, Robert L. | 1620 McVicar, Topeka, Kan. | 24 |
| Blair, John N. | 809 NW 39th, Oklahoma City, Okla. | 102 |
| Bledsoe, Chester R. | Death Field, Va. | 29 |
| Bliss, E. L. | 2641 Blanche, Pasadena, Calif. | 61 |
| Bloom, Wilford A. | Rt. 1, Capron, Ill. | 93 |
| Blum, Leander N. | Box 64, Earling, Iowa | 11 |
| Boch, Francis | 558 E. Walnut, Lancaster, Ohio | 68 |
| Boehmer, Burton F. | 1116 McCleary, McKeesport, Pa. | 33 |
| Boerngen, Frank | 1427 Rolland, Canton, Ohio | 11 |
| Bohne, Edward C. | Chicago, Ill. | 33 |
| Bohr, Benjamin | 1021 Fort, Honolulu, T. H. | 95 |
| Boice, Fred D., Jr. | 2410 Carey, Cheyene, Wyo. | 24 |
| Boller, Robert | Des Moines, Iowa | 95 |
| Bonavita, Anthony, Jr. | 224 Elm, Newark, N. J. | 107 |
| Bongo, Nick | 71 St. Marys, Nutley, N. J. | 32 |
| Bonish, Leo S. | 1405 N. Patterson Pk., Baltimore, Md. | 103 |
| Bontea, George J. | 1814-8th, Canton, Ohio | 61 |
| Borchardt, George | 655 S. Myrtle, Kankakee, Ill. | 61 |
| Borg, Delmar E. | Porter, Ind. | 34 |
| Bosco, Sebastian B. | Niagara Falls, N. Y. | 77 |
| Bosley, Lloyd L. | 3644 W. 109th, Inglewood, Calif. | 102 |
| Boswell, Milton B. | Oscala, Fla. | 11 and 95 |
| Botlik, Frank J. | 1421 E. 7th, Shawnee, Okla. | 84 |
| Boyer, Robert E. | 220 S. Arlington, Springfield, Ohio | 82 |
| Boyer, William R. | Lake Park, Iowa | 25 |
| Boyle, W. D. | 2641½ N. Spaulding, Chicago, Ill. | 61 |
| Bradshaw, R. G. | 503 S. Pleasant, Royal Oak, Mich. | 60 |
| Bramlett, Thomas B. | 6 Gordon, Roanoke, Ala. | 63 |
| Brandes, Roy W. | 2621 Allen, Indianapolis, Ind. | 91 |
| Branson, Charles N. | Washington, D. C. | 87 |
| Bratcher, Douglas H. | Monroe City, Tex. | 99 |
| Breen, Robert N. | 3859 W. 135th, Cleveland, Ohio | 90 |
| Breene, Robert G., Jr. | | 97 |
| Bregar, Adolph | 2498 Edwin, Akron, Ohio | 32 and 93 |
| Breiter, Bernard J. | Church, Bensenville, Ill. | 42 |
| Brendle, Lee E. | 3104-3rd, San Diego, Calif. | 33 |
| Brenneman, Walter J. | 1078 Seymour, Columbus, Ohio | 92 |
| Bricker, Glenn W. | 1101 W. Wyoming, Philadelphia, Pa. | 11 |
| Bricker, Lyle E. | 3104 Lincoln, Alameda, Calif. | 29 |
| Bridge, Arthur H. | Carnelian, RFD, Cucamonga, Calif. | 102 |
| Bridges, Harold W. | 838 Broadway, New Orleans, La. | 77 |
| Bridgman, Richard H. | Denver, Colo. | 11 |
| Brightwell, Earl L. | 804 First, Moultrie, Ga. | 27 |
| Brink, Gene | 689 S. Richardson, Columbus, Ohio | 25 |
| Brinker, Charles W. | 1218 Spruce, Easton, Pa. | 66 |

| NAME — ADDRESS | PAGE |
|---|---|
| Brinkworth, Richard—New York, N. Y. | 74 |
| Broadway, Margaret E.—1011 Union, Lafayette, Ind. | 64 |
| Brock, John W.—808 N. 22nd, Quincy, Ill. | 103 |
| Brock, Thomas—326 Medford, Malden, Mass. | 35 |
| Brodeth, Joseph—Manila, P. I. | 12 |
| Brodie, Ference J.—Bedford, Mass. | 67 |
| Broemer, Herbert O.—Rt. 4, San Antonio, Tex. | 85 |
| Brooks, Rand—Santa Monica, Calif. | 91 |
| Brosch, E. F.—602 Navahoe, Detroit, Mich. | 60 |
| Brothers, Luther—201 N. 11th, Wilmington, N. C. | 21 |
| Brown, Arthur—Rt. 1, Ashton, Ill. | 31 |
| Brown, Clarence A., Jr.—309 Keyes, Watertown, N. Y. | 103 |
| Brown, Davage—205 S. Plain, Ithica, N. Y. | 27 |
| Brown, Kenneth M.—553 Third, Salt Lake City, Utah | 11 |
| Brown, Robert L.—Paris, Tex. | 93 |
| Brown, Wesley E.—Box 1231, Tyona, Calif. | 31 |
| Bruner, C. E.—South Gate, Calif. | 61 |
| Brusseau, Paul A.—716 Fourth, Hayward, Calif. | 21 |
| Buatt, Joe L.—111 E. 10th, Crowley, La. | 92 |
| Bucholz, Clarence J.—Perham, Minn. | 68 |
| Buck, Howard W.—3416 Walnut, Chicago, Ill. | 91 |
| Bullock, Richard M.—Box 596, Wenatchee, Wash. | 93 |
| Burden, Foy L.—Rt. 2, Abilene, Tex. | 33 |
| Burdick, Orlo—Brooks, Bloomsville, N. Y. | 24 |
| Burke, Chester L.—Pontiac, Mich. | 103 |
| Burke, Thomas E.—124 Lewis, Salem, Va. | 11 and 95 |
| Burkett, Joe—5404 Terry, Dallas, Tex. | 74 |
| Burns, (Lt. Col.)—1106 Lorrain, Austin, Tex. | 25 |
| Burr, Warren A.—3096 Sierra Way, San Bernardino, Calif. | 37 |
| Burtok, Dan—909 Soles, McKeesport, Pa. | 46 |
| Burtschi, Martin J.—918 Kansas, Chickasha, Okla. | 66 |
| Burton, Max L.—British Columbia, Canada | 93 |
| Bussard, William N.—Buchanan, Mich. | 67 |
| Bussey, Ralph E.—329 E. Sixth, Roswell, N. M. | 92 |
| Bustle, W. C.—RR, Hudson, Ill. | 92 |
| Busuttil, Anthony J.—3023 Bouch, Bronx, N. Y. | 34 |
| Butterfield, Mason—9 S. State, Concord, N. H. | 26 |
| Byles, Ross C.—417 New 2nd, Natchitoches, La. | 14 |
| Byram, Beth June—Decatur, Neb. | 64 and 65 |
| Byrne, James F.—358 Sunset, Aurora, Ill. | 21 |
| Bywater, Murray A.—2471 S. 13th E., Salt Lake City, Utah | 100 |

### C

| NAME — ADDRESS | PAGE |
|---|---|
| Calabrese, Peter A.—133 Pico, Santa Monica, Calif. | 34 |
| Cameron, Charles E. R.—Rt. 1, McAllen, Tex. | 85 |
| Cameron, Charles J.—Box 175, Waialua, Oahu, T. H. | 32 and 103 |
| Campbell, Bruce S., Jr.—579 Woodbine, Towson, Md. | 102 |
| Campbell, Dale W.—Cambridge, Iowa | 92 |
| Campbell, Robert N.—Box 18, Plattsburg, Ohio | 102 |
| Cannon, Thomas D., Jr.—439 E. Third, Cincinnati, Ohio | 92 |
| Canovsky, Nathan—5531 Willow, New Orleans, La. | 12 |
| Caponi, Vincent P.—4651 Mt. Elliott, Detroit, Mich. | 25 |
| Caputo, Joseph H. Box 229, Rt. 1, San Jose, Calif. | 60 |
| Carducci, Pat—5 Canal, Lambertville, N. J. | 76 |
| Carey, Robert F. Jr.—204 Court, Riverhead, N. Y. | 101 |
| Carleton, W. E.—2175 Maine, Long Beach, Calif. | 46 |
| Carlock, Clay R.—1001 N. Ainsworth, Tacoma, Wash. | 93 |
| Carozza, Michell—212 Charles, Waterbury, Conn. | 33 |
| Carpenter, David P.—2849 Lafayette, St. Louis, Mo. | 36 |
| Carr, Lawrence J.—Chicago, Ill. | 97 |
| Carter, Arthur B.—506 N. Main, Anna, Ill. | 84 |
| Carter, Lee I.—Cook, Neb. | 68 |
| Carwane, Anthony P.—2002-46th, Astoria, L. I., N. Y. | 84 |
| Catanzaro, Michael W.—107-53rd, Brooklyn, N. Y. | 21 |
| Caylor, Donald K.—1451 Irving, Wisconsin Rapids, Wis. | 11 |
| Cecil, Everett C.—Main, Wagoner, Okla. | 34 and 74 |
| Celeste, George—3655 Zola, San Diego, Calif. | 63 |
| Chafee, William H.—5025 Akron, Philadelphia, Pa. | 32 |
| Chalfant, J. C.—411 S. Main, Bluffton, Ind. | 92 |
| Chamberlin, Henry R.—208 Bank, Seymour, Conn. | 93 |
| Chapin, A. F.—712 N. 32nd, Waco, Tex. | 60 |
| Chapman, Sephalon—Rt. 2, Lyon, Miss. | 66 |
| Charlton, Wilfred A., Jr.—510 Roxford, So., Syracuse, N. Y. | 34 |
| Chasteen, Keith B.—308 Ash, Duncan, Okla. | 33 |
| Cherr, Irving—897 Albany, Brooklyn, N. Y. | 11 |
| Cherrington, Don C.—91 Hough, Lafayette, Calif. | 11 |
| Chesnel, A. E.—Sanford, Me. | 18 and 99 |
| Chiappinelli, Elia A.—9 Mountain, Mt. Kisco, N. Y. | 37 |
| Chong, Gee—926 Allertown, Bronx, N. Y. | 76 and 107 |
| Chopyk, John—905 S. Springfield, Clifton Hgts, Pa. | 14 |
| Church, John C. | 93 |
| Cienski, Frank—207-05 48th, Bayside, L. I., N. Y. | 60 |
| Clark, Earl—122 State, Eldorado, Ill. | 36 |
| Clark, Kenneth E.—Miami, Fla. | 87 |
| Clark, L. D.—1607 S. Salina, Syracuse, N. Y. | 11 |
| Clark, L. G.—Walhalla, S. C. | 24 |
| Clarkson, G. A.—5760 Hamilton, Detroit, Mich. | 60 |
| Clayton, Willie G.—Stem, N. C. | 90 |
| Clein, Maurice J.—121 S. Menard, Chicago, Ill. | 31 |
| Clemencig, Arthur J.—2222 7th Ave., So. Great Falls, Mont. | 18 and 21 |
| Clinch, Leo F.—Greeley, Neb. | 21 |
| Cobb, Allen H.—1393 York, San Francisco, Calif. | 14 |
| Cochran, Paul D.—721 W. 11th, Hutchinson, Kan. | 45 |
| Cockerham, James H.—St. Louis, Mo. | 67 |
| Coffey, Stephen J.—Hartford, Conn. | 42 |
| Coffindaffer, Sam W.—RFD, Kincheloe, W. Va. | 34 |
| Cohn, Martin B.—Bronx, N. Y. | 70 |
| Colacino, Charles—233 E. Miller, Newark, N. Y. | 36 |
| Coldwell, James R.—Rt. 2, Mt. Gilead, Ohio | 63 and 92 |
| Colecchia, Theodore—1445 N. Luna, Chicago, Ill. | 76 |
| Coleman, John E.—1817 Pointview, Youngstown, Ohio | 32 |
| Collins, Wilbur E.—15 Water, Galena, Kan. | |
| Collison, Peter E.—Rt. 7, Minneapolis, Minn. | 33 and 34 |
| Conner, J. H.—Free Acres, Scotch Plains, N. J. | 11 |
| Cook, Gerald A.—3716 Lincoln, Detroit, Mich. | 83 |
| Cook, James J.—Leesville, S. C. | 24 |
| Cook, Kenneth E.—c/o LaGrange Ntnl., Bank, Zeigler, Ill. | 93 |

| NAME — ADDRESS | PAGE |
|---|---|
| Coons, Joseph D.—1295 Rademacker, Detroit, Mich. | 31 |
| Cooper, Luther D.—Laredo, Md. | 95 |
| Copeland, Howell S., Jr.—Atlanta, Ga. | 87 |
| Corocoran, John W., Jr. | 26 |
| Cosline, Hugh L., Jr.—Spruce Acre, Coddington, Ithaca, N. Y. | 67 |
| Costa, J. F.—7 Thompson, Monson, Mass. | 61 |
| Courtney, Jack L.—3 Pierce Ct., Appleton, Wis. | 108 |
| Cowart, Floyd C., Jr.—1039 SW 5th, Miami, Fla. | 21 |
| Cowgill, Thomas—3315 Bach, Cincinnati, Ohio | 31 |
| Cox, Camet—Box 92, Independence, Va. | 85 |
| Cox, E. C.—Goldfinch, Tex. | 61 |
| Cox, H. M.—922 West End, Knoxville, Tenn. | 107 |
| Cox, Leon A.—Rt. 4, Johnson City, Tenn. | 93 |
| Cox, William S.—West Point, Va. | 92 |
| Coyle, Norman—95 Duane, Ingram, Pa. | 36 |
| Craft, Orris W.—Juniata, Pa. | 90 |
| Cramer, Gail E.—Morley, Mich. | 101 |
| Crampton, Walter F.—2716 Home, Dayton, Ohio | 36 |
| Crane, Edwin R.—1112 N. Market, Wichita, Kan. | 90 |
| Craner, Francis L.—RFD No 4, Fulton, N. Y. | 92 |
| Cranford, Charles N.—34 S. Burgess, Columbus, Ohio | 63 |
| Crawford, J. P., Jr.—c/o S. E. Albin, Foosland, Ill. | 83 |
| Crawford, John M.—Ida Grove, Iowa. | 87 |
| Creany, Robert L.—1107 Greenmount, Baltimore, Md. | 27 |
| Crim, Arthur—38K Flavet Vill., Univ., of Fla., Gainesville, Fla. | 102 |
| Crist, William D.—97 W. Longview, Columbus, Ohio | 36 |
| Crockett, David E.—Roanoke, Va. | 95 |
| Crook, Donald—Revonah Pike, Liberty, N. Y. | 31 and 82 |
| Crum, Olen E. | 34 |
| Cruver, Robert K.—155 Prospect, Bound Brook, N. J. | 92 |
| Csizmadia, Joseph—Buffalo, N. Y. | 46 |
| Cubley, Rex—219 S. 12th, Durant, Okla. | 25 |
| Cullinan, Joseph—394 Beacon, Lowell, Mass. | 85 |
| Culnan, T. J.—5257 W. Iowa, Chicago, Ill. | 61 |
| Culver, Harrison—107 N. Traub, Indianapolis, Ind. | 102 |
| Cunningham, Robert M.—Beaver City, Neb. | 27 |
| Currier, Oral A.—Rt. 1, Wyaconda, Mo. | 67 |

### D

| NAME — ADDRESS | PAGE |
|---|---|
| Daly, Charles T.—530 W. 178th, New York, N. Y. | 18 and 21 |
| Dameron, Wayne G.—5005 S. Pine, Tacoma, Wash. | 25 |
| Danner, John E.—118 McQueen, Sumter, S. C. | 102 |
| Danylo, Michael—110-3rd, Koppel, Pa. | 93 |
| Darman, Richard B.—225 W. Rosedale, Ft. Worth, Tex. | 66 |
| Daugherty, Jesse J.—Elvins, Mo. | 15 and 34 |
| Dauginas, John D.—10712 S. Wabash, Chicago, Ill. | 33 |
| Davenport, Willard—Rt. 1, Brookland, Ark. | 24 |
| Davids, Charles E.—900 River, Troy, N. Y. | 24 |
| Davids, Jack—2908 Holly, Seattle, Wash. | 20 |
| Davies, Harold A.—3001 Knowlson, Pittsburgh, Pa. | 24 |
| Davis, Gene L.—Mortons Gap, Ky. | 45 and 68 |
| Davis, Richard S.—236 S. Linden, Beverly Hills, Calif. | 32 |
| Davis, Robert C.—612 S. Smithville, Dayton, Ohio | 93 |
| Davis, Samuel J.—19 Neptune, Lynn, Mass. | 24 |
| Davis, W. V., Jr.—Savannah, Ga. | 24 |
| Day, John C.—Lee Theater, Richmond, Va. | 84 |
| Dean, E. E.—Norman, Okla. | 61 |
| DeBoer, Peter, Jr.—Ellsworth, Minn. | 75, 77 and 87 |
| Decker, Clyde N.—Rt. 1, Cornell, Calif. | 102 |
| DeGrio, Pat—2 N. 100th West, Duluth, Minn. | 84 |
| Delago, Angel—642 Penns, San Francisco, Calif. | 61 |
| Delhom, Earnest M. | 26 |
| Dell, John F.—5226 Baufort, Baltimore, Md. | 12 |
| Delong, Robert F.—101 Northwood, Syracuse, N. Y. | 21 |
| DeMent, Leon N.—2355 E. Mason, Baton Rouge, La. | 25 |
| Denison, Frank | 26 |
| DeSantis, Patrick J.—Carteret, N. J. | 77 |
| Descheny, Keyah—Rock Point Store, Chin Lee, Ariz. | 93 |
| Detalia, William—933 E. 32nd, Brooklyn, N. Y. | 46 |
| Dete, C. A.—20 E. Dartmore, Akron, Ohio | 11 |
| Detlof, S. F.—4745 S. Marshfield, Chicago, Ill. | 61 |
| Deutsch, Frederick M.—5503 Merville, Baltimore, Md. | 92 |
| DeVault, Ralph E.—RR 5, Shelbyville, Ind. | 84 |
| Devereaux, Ray W.—Rt. 2, Pascagoula, Miss. | 105 |
| DeVona, Joseph J.—1001 Avery, Syracuse, N. Y. | 24 |
| Dibble, Edward H.—319 Garrard, Rantoul, Ill. | 92 |
| Dickinson, Wayne E. | 63 |
| Dietz, Raymond A. | 63 |
| Divis, Theodore J.—Wahoo, Neb. | 82 |
| Doam, Robert S.—528 Fourth, LaSalle, Ill. | 25 |
| Doherty (Hanna), Madeline S.—85 Hill St., Norwood, Mass. | 65 |
| Dolan, Joseph—524 Georgia, Chattanooga, Tenn. | 85 |
| Domres, Gordon F.—3303 N. Richard, Milwaukee, Wis. | 92 |
| Donohue, John R.—Couderay, Wis. | 25 |
| Dool, John H.—Lamar, Mo. | 48 |
| Dooling, John A.—151 Lorraine, Mt. Vernon, N. Y. | 101 |
| Doolittle, James | 96 |
| Doose, Keith I.—Belden, Neb. | 66 |
| Dorais, Frederick E., Jr.—Akron, Ohio | 108 |
| Dorn, John | 26 |
| Doto, Vincent F.—369 N. 7th, Newark, N. J. | 18 and 21 |
| Douglas, Robert W. Jr.—Fort Slocum, New Rochelle, N. Y. | 46, 96 & 97 |
| Douel, Robert J.—9101 Ave. K, Brooklyn, N. Y. | 92 |
| Dove, Louis H.—Rt. 1, Ward, Ark. | 70 |
| Dowden, Milton—Waterloo, Iowa. | 67 |
| Down, Robert R.—4528 Zane, Los Angeles, Calif. | 102 |
| Doxey (Heffernan) Georgia O.—Rt. 1, El Centro, Calif. | 64 |
| Doyle, Howard—1438 Cypress, Paris, Ky. | 24 |
| Drinnen, Cecil C.—2819 Linden, Knoxville, Tenn. | 45 and 90 |
| Druliner, Roger L.—1600 "O" St., Lincoln, Neb. | 107 |
| DuBois, Rene—219 Play, Carey, Ohio. | 61 |
| Duerschmidt, Wayne A.—1255 Cherry, Green Bay, Wis. | 25 |
| Duerr, Richard D.—2300-3rd, Sacramento, Calif. | 6 and 7 |
| Dugan, Laurence | 63 |
| Dugdale, Wendall—765 E. 17th, Salt Lake City, Utah. | 84 |
| Durham, Sheldon D.—1512 Spruce, Minneapolis, Minn. | 46 |
| Durrett, John J.—Cumberland, Md. | 70 |

| NAME | ADDRESS | PAGE |
|---|---|---|
| Dyer, R. W. | 852 Blaine, Pontiac, Mich. | 61 |
| Dyer, Theodore M. | Stetson Rd., Hanover, Mass. | 92 |
| Dyson, James W. | Box 37, Lanai City, T. H. | 24 |
| Dziadusa, E. F. | 120 Market, Garfield, N. J. | 60 |

### E

| NAME | ADDRESS | PAGE |
|---|---|---|
| Eaton, F. C. | Roanoke, Va. | 37 |
| Ebeling, Harry | 314 N. Ford, Fullerton, Calif. | 26 |
| Echard, Willard L. | | 63 |
| Eckhart, Leslie E. | 1268 Wyoming, Forty Fort, Pa. | 33 |
| Eddy, Raymond | 933 W. 18th, Los Angeles, Calif. | 85 |
| Eden, Ralph | Box 57, Osseo, Minn. | 20 |
| Edlkraut, Edward C. | 16 Doremus, Clifton, N. J. | 34 |
| Edmonds, Frank | 321 W. Currahee, Poccoa, Ga. | 58 |
| Edwards, Bob | Westfield, Ind. | 21 |
| Edwards, Lloyd C. | Box 3022, HAAF, Hobbs, N. M. | 101 |
| Edwards, Paul N. | 1859 York, Denver, Colo. | 92 |
| Eldridge, Jim C. | Albuquerque, N. M. | 46 |
| Eliopouslos, William | 440 Mass, Cambridge, Mass. | 21 |
| Elliot, Bill R. | 505 W. Spring, Neosho, Mo. | 24 |
| Elliott, William | 1355 W. 95th, Cleveland, Ohio. | 84 |
| Ellis, Jewell P. | Rt. 1, Tyronza, Ark. | 64 and 65 |
| Ellis, Lexie L. | Braggadocio, Mo. | 34 |
| Elmer, Carlos | | 85 |
| Emig, Carl J. | 138-02 14th, College Point, N. Y. | 82 |
| Emilio, Albert | 58 Stillman, Westerly, R. I. | 21 |
| Engram, Thomas B. | 1209 N. Monroe, Johnson City, Ill. | 93 |
| Enman, Carver | 200 Wildwood, Worcester, Mass. | 20 |
| Ennis, Francis L. | 1115 N. Fuller, Hollywood, Calif. | 101 |
| Enochs, Maurice W. | 415 E. Washington, Sullivan, Ind. | 21 |
| Erbele, Fred C. | 20 W. Jenkintown, Glenside, Pa. | 25 |
| Espinosa, Efrain T. | New York, N. Y. | 32 |
| Essler, Gordon J. | 18 Railroad, Beverly, Mass. | 36 |
| Estes, Alfred | 3214 Cliff, Birmingham, Ala. | 92 |
| Estep, Wilmer M. | Maysel, W. Va. | 61 |
| Esthman, H.R. | 1512 Adams, Huntington, W. Va. | 61 |
| Evans, James A. | | 34 |
| Eyre, Vern B. | Rawlins, Wyo. | 87 |

### F

| NAME | ADDRESS | PAGE |
|---|---|---|
| Fager, Loren V. | 241 Vermejo, Raton, N. M. | 20 |
| Fahey, Joseph H., Jr. | 717 Hope, Springdale, Conn. | 101 |
| Fahnstock, Edward | 625 Judy, Bridgeport, Ill. | 64 |
| Faile, Ray | 908 Selma, Mobile, Ala. | 83 |
| Faltemier, Edward W. | St. Marie, Ill. | 38 |
| Fannon, Floyd M. | Box 1033, Cody, Wyo. | 45 and 68 |
| Farischon, Gerald | 1301 Somerset, Pekin, Ill. | 36 |
| Farrington, Charles S. | High Point, N. C. | 27 |
| Farry, James N. | 415 Pa., Schenectady, N. Y. | 36 |
| Feduson, Ralph | Union City, Okla. | 102 |
| Feickert, Robert H. | 204-6th, NW, Mandon, N.D. | 20 and 21 |
| Fender, Thomas H. | 900 Kentucky, Amarillo, Tex. | 77 |
| Fergus, D. E. | 419 Emily, Anaheim, Calif. | 61 |
| Ferguson, J. P. | Box 21, Rocky, Okla. | 61 |
| Ferguson, Robert L. | Chicago, Ill. | 37 |
| Ferling, Jack | | 63 |
| Ferris, Roy S. | Kinde, Mich. | 36 |
| Feskun, Luke | 203 Scoville, Buffalo, N. Y. | 26 |
| Fiechtinger, Edward | | 63 |
| Finnie, Harold F. | 1585-36th, Oakland, Calif. | 63 |
| Fischer, Charles | 9311 Old Bonhomme, Clayton, Mo. | 61 |
| Fischer, Clyde M. | 426 W. 14th, Centralia, Ill. | 12 |
| Fisher, William J. | Berrian Pl., Port Chester, N. Y. | 101 |
| Flaherty, Agnes E. | 34-58 74th St., Jackson Hts., N. Y. | 64 and 65 |
| Flanagan, Henry G. | 3228 40th, Meridian, Miss. | 105 |
| Fleming, Elsie Nolan | Middletown, Mo. | 64, 65 and 75 |
| Flood, William J. | 3512 Mass., NW, Washington, D. C. | 97 |
| Floyd, Richard | 49 N. Morris, Newark, Ohio. | 102 |
| Flynn, A. I. | 1706 Foothill, Lavergne, Calif. | 24 |
| Foore, David R. | 1452 Farris, Fresno, Calif. | 29 and 74 |
| Ford, Ralph W. | Corpus Christi, Tex. | 15 |
| Formosa, F. | 1260 Plum, San Jose, Calif. | 85 |
| Fosbach, Christian | Cushman, Ore. | 24 |
| Fosburg, Hugh W. | Cherry Plain, N. Y. | 99 |
| Foulke, Forrest K. | Box 123, Leucadia, Calif. | 21 |
| Fowler, Melvin C. | Rt. 1, Bankston, Ala. | 33 |
| Fox, Theodore H. | 1547 Macauley, Cleveland, Ohio. | 93 |
| Franco, Leone V. | | 95 |
| Frank, Arthur L. | 436 S. River, Wilkes-Barre, Pa. | 36 |
| Frank, John D. | 946 Wellington, Chicago, Ill. | 92 |
| Franklin, Harry | Box 451, Dawson, Okla. | 33 |
| Fredericks, Benjamin M. | Rt. 5, Winterset, Iowa. | 84 |
| Freedman, Edward | 1628 Colombia, Chicago, Ill. | 27 |
| Freedman, Joseph J. | 513 S. Warren, Trenton, N. J. | 90 |
| Freeland, Robin | | 63 |
| Freeman, E. M. | 1642 Tabor, Indianapolis, Ind. | 61 |
| Freeman, Wallace M. | Dayton Bluff, Sta. No. 4, St. Paul, Minn. | 92 |
| Freligh, William P. | 2301 Sturtevant, Detroit, Mich. | 82 |
| Frey, William C. | 2409 Walnut, Harrisburg, Pa. | 25 |
| Fridley, Jerry D. | | 63 |
| Frokjer, Ivan C. | Rt. 1, Luck, Wis. | 36 and 82 |
| Frum, C. O. | S. Sioux City, Neb. | 61 |
| Frye, Gerald L. | Dallas, Tex. | 68 and 69 |
| Frye, Melton | 3126 Cluckner, Lincoln, Neb. | 36 |
| Furge, John | 1406 Anderson, Bristol, Tenn. | 101 |

### G

| NAME | ADDRESS | PAGE |
|---|---|---|
| Gailey, James | | 34 |
| Gaines, Royal C. | 4836 NE Everett, Portland, Ore. | 77 |
| Gainey, Andrew G. | 3337 Federal, Denver, Colo. | 91 |
| Gaither, Gant | 1704 S. Main, Hopkinsville, Ky. | 91 |
| Galello, Armando V. | 26 Barnhart, N. Tarrytown, N. Y. | 33 |
| Gallagher, Frank M., Jr. | Carnation Farms, Carnation, Wash. | 35 |
| Gamache, Albert C. | 2503 Wetherburn, Baltimore, Md. | 102 |
| Gamble, Benjamin L. | Rt. 1, Bolivar, Pa. | 11 |
| Gannon, William B. | Cleveland, Ohio. | 42 |
| Garbarino, Paul | Box 297, Oberlin, La. | 76 |
| Garcia, John M. | Rt. 2, Box 344, Hollister, Calif. | 11 |
| Garland, John R. | 85 Dunnell, Pawtucket, R. I. | 95 |
| Garner, Kathleen | Gay, Ga. | 11 |
| Gartner, George C. | 1140 Esperanza, San Bernadino, Calif. | 25 |
| Gassell, Harry | 1579 Park, Camden, N. J. | 87 |
| Gates, J. S. | Box 101, LaPryor, Tex. | 61 |
| Geffel, John | 699-2nd, Beaver, Pa. | 17 |
| Geise, John | RR 4, Box 400, Richmond, Ind. | 36 |
| Gendreau, Donald W. | 70 Doncaster, Henrietta, N. Y. | 37 |
| Gentry, Howard N. | Montgomery City, Mo. | 107 |
| Gerres, Herman | Rock Springs, Mo. | 67 |
| Giaguinto, Chick | Bronx, N. Y. | 77 |
| Giansiracusa, Sebastiano R. | Box 117, Niagara Univ. PO. N. Y. | 31 |
| Gibson, Lloyd B. | 137 N. 14th, Olean, N. Y. | 31 |
| Gibson, W. W. | 3203 W. Gadsden, Pensacola, Fla. | 77 |
| Gilchrist, Charles W. | 704 N. Gay, Mt. Vernon, Ohio. | 95 |
| Giles, Barnie M | | 96 and 97 |
| Gilger, G. P. | Burkburnett, Texas | 60 |
| Gillen, J. M. | 940-10th, Cedar Rapids, Iowa. | 61 |
| Gilmore, Harrison | Toledo, Ohio. | 84 |
| Gilstad, Lyle | Grand View, Wis. | 102 |
| Ginsburg, B. | 2641 Euclid, Detroit, Mich. | 24 |
| Giordano, Rocco P. | 520-18th, Brooklyn, N. Y. | 27 |
| Giullo, Antonello | 4 Prince, Boston, Mass. | 29 |
| Glassburn, R. D. | Rt. 1, Box 216, Fortville, Ind. | 61 |
| Gleason, John | 80 Kenneth, Santa Cruz, Calif. | 20 |
| Goch, Cecil R. | Rt. 1, Prospect, Tenn. | 95 |
| Gonterman, A. F. | 1325 N. Fourth, Evansville, Ind. | 25 |
| Gonterman, Earl C. | | 95 |
| Goode, Mike W. | 1110 Wilmer, Anaston, Ala. | 60 |
| Goodrich, Fred | Harriman, Tenn. | 103 |
| Gooley, Marshall J. | 1305 W. Sunnyside, Chicago, Ill. | 31 |
| Gordon, Avery W. | 9360 Genessee, Detroit, Mich. | 102 |
| Gorski, Joe | 8019 Medina, Cleveland, Ohio. | 67 |
| Gotwals, Jacob W. | 251 N. Bundy, Los Angeles, Calif. | 93 |
| Gorsky, Eddie | 225 Main, Springville, N. Y. | 21 |
| Goul, William W. | Box 657, Muncie, Ind. | 20 |
| Graupner, Roy E. | Box 158 Newport, Wash. | 87 |
| Gray, Edward E. | R. G. LeTorneau, Inc. Longview, Tex. | 93 |
| Gray, George | RFD 2, Caledonia, Ohio. | 60 |
| Gray, Lucien | Nisbel, Wash. | 11 |
| Gray, Richard L. | Broadway Hotel, Sand Springs, Okla. | 84 |
| Grayner, Lewis T. | 133 Hawaii, NE, Washington, D. C. | 31 |
| Green, Samuel M. | 165 Sherman, Fort Thomas, Ky. | 24 |
| Green | | 97 |
| Greenman, Allyn | Chaplin, Conn. | 17 |
| Greenwald, Peter | Detroit, Mich. | 77 |
| Gregory, H. Franklin | 1317 Raleigh, Dayton, Ohio. | 93 |
| Grimaldi, Patrick J. | 755 Park, Brooklyn, N. Y. | 77 |
| Grishaber, R. S. | 1004 W. 104th, Chicago, Ill. | 61 |
| Gross, Leonard B. | 668 Waller, San Francisco, Calif. | 32 |
| Grosse, Otto | Dover, N. J. | 17 |
| Grossman, James M. | 6101 Sheridan, Chicago, Ill. | 27 |
| Grover, Fred T. | 2735 Stuart, Berkeley, Calif. | 102 |
| Grunewald, E. J. | 1447 W. Summit, San Antonio, Tex. | 15 |
| Gugliotta, Johnny | 719-17th, Ensley, Birmingham, Ala. | 27 |
| Guinnee, R. P. | 310 S. State, Bloomington, Ill. | 39 |
| Gunn, Richard L. | Detroit, Mich. | 29 |
| Guyette, Abraham | 68 Cottage, Easthampton, Mass. | 20 |

### H

| NAME | ADDRESS | PAGE |
|---|---|---|
| Haas, Harold R. | Kiana, Alaska | 33 |
| Haertel, David | 5588 Angle, Greendale, Wis. | 93 |
| Hagen, Harold M. | 516 Jersey, Joliet, Ill. | 107 |
| Hagood, Thomas D. | Albertville, Ala. | 63 |
| Hale, Willis | Hq. 4th AF, San Francisco, Cal. | 15, 24, 96, 97 |
| Hallmann, Don C. | Evansville, Ind. | 42 |
| Hall, Phillip | Rt. 1, Box 221, Springfield, Ore. | 34 |
| Hamelton, D. F. | 414 N. 8th, Keokuk, Iowa | 61 |
| Hamilton, George E. | | 63 |
| Hamilton, John W. | | 63 |
| Hamilton, William A. | 2345 Fulton, Berkley, Calif. | 11 |
| Hammar, Roy | 316 E. 112th, Los Angeles, Calif. | 24 |
| Hankins, C. P. | 413 E. Polk, Harlingen, Tex. | 60 |
| Hanson, Clifford T. | 215 East St., Hobart, Ind. | 85 |
| Harakal, John J., Jr. | 111-3rd, Hokendauqua, Pa. | 74 |
| Harbour, Earl H. | Memphis, Tenn. | 93 |
| Hardy, Robert J. | 903 Burgandy, Baltimore, Md. | 34 |
| Harker, Malcolm H. | Healdton, Okla. | 66 |
| Harmon, Millard F. | | 38, 96, 97 and 99 |
| Harrell, Turner | Petersburg, Va. | 16 |
| Harris, Aster A. | 34 River, Cliff Side, N. C. | 77 |
| Harris, D. W. | Birmingham, Ill. | 61 |
| Harris, James | 4558 Prarie, Chicago, Ill. | 11 |
| Harris, J. W. | 616 Lagro, LeMay, Mo. | 60 |
| Harris, Madelyn | Box 196, Peabody Col., Nashville, Tenn. | 64, 65 |
| Harris, Robert J. | 202-8th, Rockport, Ind. | 24 |
| Hartman, Harry P. | Kansas City, Mo. | 67 |
| Hartman, Ralph F | Santa Rosa Hosp., San Antonio, Tex. | 26 |
| Hasledalen, Robert N. | Carpio, N. D. | 92 |
| Haslett, Perry E. | 1309 S. 4th, Maywood, Ill. | 99 |
| Hass, William W. | 501 S. Central, Chino, Calif. | 11 |
| Hatfield, Kenneth R. | Colcord, W. Va. | 33 |
| Haubrich, Rob. | 1745 King, Columbus, Ohio. | 21 |
| Hayes, Carlton F. | Rt. 1, Douglasville, Ga. | 20 |
| Hayes, Peter L. | Los Angeles, Calif. | 91 |
| Haysel, George R. | 1746 N. Bronson, Los Angeles, Calif. | 93 |
| Haywood, Clayton | HQ &BS Sq., March Field, Calif. | 31 |
| Headley, Marvin | Rt. 5, Clanton, Ala. | 83 |
| Heap, Elizabeth | 516 Maynard, Knoxville, Tenn. | 90 |
| Heckendorf, Howard A. | 4988 N. Kolmar, Chicago, Ill. | 29 and 74 |
| Hedgren, Jens G. | 5366 Winthrop, Chicago, Ill. | 93 |
| Hedstrom, Eric L. | River St., Norwell, Mass. | 90 |
| Hegy, Clarence | Hartford, Wis. | 20 |
| Heisey, Harold S. | 237 N. Lime, Lancaster, Pa. | 24 |
| Hellekson, Willard D. | 421 Mound, Mankato, Minn. | 27 |
| Heller, Glenn F. | 238 W. Penn, Muncy, Pa. | 24 |
| Henckell, Herbert N. | Cairo, Ill. | 25 |

| NAME | ADDRESS | PAGE |
|---|---|---|
| Hendricks, Edgar E.—Birmingham, Ala. | | 17 |
| Herbig, Andrew W.—1775 Sycamore, Cincinnati, Ohio. | | 29 |
| Herlin, K. A.—6816 Clyde, Chicago, Ill. | | 61 |
| Herriott, Richard M.—607 Frost, San Antonio, Tex. | | 24 |
| Herrling, Stanley—Washington, D. C. | | 11 |
| Herschberger, Vernon Q.—Box 21, Harper, Kan. | | 31 |
| Hersh, Raymond—Rt. 1, Mertztown, Pa. | | 90 |
| Hewett, Mrs. Harry—Honolulu, T. H. | | 11 |
| Hibbs, David W.—Richmond, Calif. | | 95 |
| Hilgenfel, Edward J.—Box 186, Henrietta, Tex. | | 25 |
| Hillman, C. C.—1334 Kappes, Indianapolis, Ind. | | 61 |
| Himmele, Irvin H.—Buffalo, N. Y. | | 11 |
| Hines, S. W.—Cumberland, Wis. | | 90 |
| Hintermeier, Richard H.—29 Washington, Kenmore, N. Y. | | 102 |
| Hintze, Milton A.—Brooklyn, N. Y. | | 11 |
| Hinz, Daniel L.—3445 S. Burrell, Milwaukee, Wis. | | 101 |
| Hittler, Andrew C.—1524 W. 11th, St. Louis, Mo. | | 33 |
| Hix, J. E—3511 Cedar Springs, Dallas, Texas. | | 60 |
| Hochevar, Frank | | 63 |
| Hockman, Lawrence J. | | 63 |
| Hoffman, Earl E.—Box 193, Grant, Neb. | | 66 |
| Hoffman, Herman R., Jr.—Wausau, Wis. | | 26 |
| Holley, Roy L.—15 AF Stat. Con. Sec., Colorado Springs, Colo. | | 105 |
| Holmes, Richard—1031 Washington, Galesburg, Ill. | | 39 |
| Holsapfel, William—HQ AAF, Pentagon, Washington, D. C. | | 18 |
| Hood, Elson B.—Dixieland 5 & 10 Stores, Nashville, Ga. | | 27 |
| Hooker, F. D.—200 S. Broadway, Redondo Beach, Calif. | | 61 |
| Hooker, Jesse M.—Falling Springs, Va. | | 77 |
| Hooper, Clyde O., Jr.—152 Grant St., Portland, Me. | | 31 |
| Hooper, Floyd M.—1803 Eastside, Nashville, Tenn. | | 46 |
| Hoover, Charles L.—420 W. Chestnut, Junction City, Kan. | | 32 |
| Hoppock, Eleanor—34-58 74th, Jackson Heights, N. Y. | | 64 |
| Hooper, Keith A.—Harrison, Ark. | | 68 |
| Horowitz, Edward | | 63 |
| Horton, Lewis T.—612 E. 8th, Metropolis, Ill. | | 20 |
| Horton, Wilford G.—Lafe, Ark. | | 90 |
| Hosens, Edwin L. | | 53 |
| Hougham, Whitney H.—1109 N. McLean, Bloomington, Ill. | | 60 |
| House, Coleman B.—11571 Sheldon, Roscoe, Calif. | | 33 |
| Howard, A. B. | | 95 |
| Howard, James P.—Andover, Ill. | | 85 |
| Howard, R. G.—903 N. Cedar, Ottawa, Kan. | | 24 |
| Hubbard, Henry W.—Olnay, Ill. | | 11 |
| Hubbard, Wilbur T.—7512-14th, SW, Seattle, Wash. | | 21 |
| Hudock, James—Smock, Pa. | | 34 |
| Huenow, Manfred—Rt. 4, San Antonio, Tex. | | 61 |
| Hueter, Charles—1901 McDuffle, Houston, Tex. | | 83 |
| Huffman, William P.—1200 Sixth, Hickory, N. C. | 36 and | 82 |
| Hughes, Glenn S.—20 Bowles, Oakland, Calif. | | 25 |
| Hughes, Robert J.—19 Bungalow Pike, Stamford, Conn. | | 83 |
| Hughes, Larry D.—78-8th, Wood Ridge, N. J. | | 34 |
| Humphries, Buford M.—420 N. Melandres, Las Cruces, N. M. | | 11 |
| Hunt, Allie B.—Commerce, Ga. | | 21 |
| Hunter, George H., Jr.—Box 202, Alta Loma, Calif. | 101 and | 102 |
| Hunter, J. C., Jr.—314 S. Lewis, LaGrange, Ga. | | 63 |
| Hunter, John A.—Henry, Ill. | | 34 |
| Hunter, W. K.—RFD 2, Utica, Ohio. | | 63 |
| Hussey, John J., Jr.—378th Fighter Sq., Lawson Field, Ft. Benning, Ga. | 25 and 39, 102 and | 103 |
| Hutchins, James L. | | 63 |
| Hutmacher, Henry E.—531 New York, Sebring, Ohio. | | 36 |
| Hyatt, John R.—Rt. 1, Dunbar, Pa. | | 74 |
| Hynes, William A.—20 Cambon, San Francisco, Calif. | | 34 |

### I

| | | |
|---|---|---|
| Iovino, Anthony F.—678 Glenmore, Brooklyn, N. Y. | | 25 |
| Irigoyen, Richard F.—806 Edgewood, Englewood, Calif. | | 24 |

### J

| | | |
|---|---|---|
| Jacobe, David—Baileys Harbor, Wis. | | 33 |
| Jaffe, Harold—1335 Coral, Brooklyn, N. Y. | | 68 |
| Jakubowski, Melvin—1522 Clement, Baltimore, Md. | | 27 |
| James, Harry W.—RD 1, Teako Rd., Box 73, Wharton, N. J. | | 25 |
| James, R. W.—11616 N. Martindale, Detroit, Mich. | | 60 |
| Jamison, A. L.—5239 Cabanne, St. Louis, Mo. | | 31 |
| Jenkins, George F.—109 Glade, Conyers, Ga. | | 26 |
| Jenkins, Ishmael—Rt. 10, Houston, Tex. | | 11 |
| Jennaro, J. H.—Texas City, Texas. | | 60 |
| Jenne, H. E.—Jamaica, N. Y. | | 24 |
| Jennings, Sam—229 Chapel, Nashville, Tenn. | | 84 |
| Johnson, Carl E., Jr.—1428 SW 12th, Portland, Ore. | | 93 |
| Johnson, C. Lawrence—529 Linden, Bethlehem, Pa. | | 17 |
| Johnson, David E.—Platte Center, Neb. | | 26 |
| Johnson, Francis—Jamaica, N. Y. | | 24 |
| Johnson, Francis M.—RFD 3, Scribner, Neb. | | 32 |
| Johnson, Frank O.—42 Heights, Fair Lawn, N. J. | | 33 |
| Johnson, Norman W.—25 University, Brookline, Mass. | | 32 |
| Johnson, W. H.—Cuero, Tex. | | 11 |
| Jones, Donald N.—2028 E. Sinto, Spokane, Wash. | | 34 |
| Jones, Edward A.—Rt. 3, Box 31, Waupaca, Wis. | | 11 |
| Jones, Floyd—Parker, Va. | | 12 |
| Jones, Fronnie A., Jr.—Box 868, New Bern, N. C. | | 102 |
| Jones, James D.—1315 E. 18th, Denver, Colo. | | 60 |
| Jones, Paul A.—3006 Blanche, Pasadena, Calif. | | 31 |
| Jones, Richard—Boston, Mass. | | 16 |
| Jones, Sara Ann—3336 N. Broad, Philadelphia, Pa. | | 64 |
| Joselson, Stan—3326 Steuben, New York, N. Y. | | 21 |

### K

| | | |
|---|---|---|
| Kaaihue, Norman—2308 North and South Rds., St. Louis, Mo. | | 91 |
| Kaempfer, Robert E.—138 Merriweather, Cape Giardeau, Mo. | | 32 |
| Kanan, Van R.—91 Main, Fremont, Ohio. | | 63 |
| Kaplan, Jacob H.—183 Chelsea, E. Boston, Mass. | | 21 |
| Kara, Elmer T.—643 N. Kennsington, Chicago, Ill. | | 100 |
| Karr, H. H.—6734 Bradley, St. Louis, Mo. | | 60 |
| Kasanov, Milton—1703 Clinton, Rochester, N. Y. | | 25 |
| Kates, Clarence S.—Glen Mill, Pa. | | 11 |

| NAME | ADDRESS | PAGE |
|---|---|---|
| Kattner, Jerome F.—313 W. Catawissa, Nesquehoning, Pa. | | 33 |
| Katz, Max—147 Lafayette, Patterson, N. J. | | 31 |
| Kearney, Emmet L.—343 Green Bay, Glencoe, Ill. | | 101 |
| Keifer, A. H.—Clendenin, W. Va. | | 61 |
| Kelly, Francis—30 Slocum, Marcellus, N. Y. | | 11 |
| Kelly, John—114 7th Ave. N., St. Petersburg, Fla. | | 76 |
| Kenningston, Milas H.—1212 Pine, Texarkana, Tex. | | 93 |
| Kenzik, J. J.—1011 E. 35th, Loraine, Ohio. | | 25 |
| Kerns, Leonard T.—Ellsworth, Kan. | | 99 |
| Kesler, Doris L.—558 English, N.W., Atlanta, Ga. | | 11 |
| Ketchum, James E.—Vinita, Okla. | | 37 |
| Killion, William F.—Reelsville, Ind. | | 101 |
| Kilmartin, Edward J., Jr.—35-12 171st, Flushing, N. Y. | | 90 |
| Kilpatrick, Harold J.—16 Columbus, Bedford, Ohio. | | 42 |
| Kimmich, William A.—126 Westwood, New Haven, Conn. | | 90 |
| King, Edward—100 Court, Reno, Nev. | | 65 |
| King, James O.—Concordi, Ky. | | 66 |
| Kirby, D. M.—550 Briar, Chicago, Ill. | | 61 |
| Kirby, William C., Jr.—306 Ponce De Leon, Decatur, Ga. | | 27 |
| Kirchhoff, Fred—353 Yale, San Antonio, Tex. | 14 and | 15 |
| Kirsis, Alice J.—32 Hawthorne, Arlington, Mass. | | 64 |
| Klein, Leonard W.—141—Lewis, Patterson, N. J. | | 31 |
| Kleinhans, Clifford—12 W. Los Animas, Colo. Springs, Colo. | | 90 |
| Kleinheider, Felix C.—Rt. 2, New Haven, Mo. | | 60 |
| Knes, Marvin—Chadwick, Ill. | | 68 |
| Knierim, George H.—221 Oriole, Rochester, N. Y. | | 31 |
| Knippa, A. W.—425 Uvalde, San Antonio, Tex. | | 61 |
| Knobloch, Edgar M.—819 E. 19th, Winfield, Kan. | | 31 |
| Koch, Kenneth L.—Box 23, Parryville, Pa. | | 60 |
| Komer, Myron—4031 Buena Vista, Detroit, Mich. | | 28 |
| Koralcik, Cyril S.—12 Vernon, Clifton, N. J. | | 91 |
| Korbos, P. T.—6852 S. Indiana, Chicago, Ill. | | 61 |
| Kornfeind, John L.—647 N. Waddell, Freeport, Ill. | | 32 |
| Korobkin, Oscar—1070 Mich., Detroit, Mich. | | 20 |
| Koropchak, Roman D.—100 Girard, Atlas, Pa. | | 84 |
| Korralski, Stanley B.—5912 Hosmer, Cleveland, Ohio. | | 25 |
| Koski, Oliver S.—Sparta Location, Eveleth, Minn. | | 14 |
| Kovaco, Emory J.—Caldwell, N. J. | | 25 |
| Kowalski, Boleslaw—7361 Sarena, Detroit, Mich. | | 102 |
| Kozak, William A.—5110 Van Horn, Elmhurst, L. I., N. Y. | | 21 |
| Krans, C. O.—1334 Fifth, Rockford, Ill. | | 25 |
| Kratzer, Harold E.—118 P. St., Salt Lake City, Utah. | | 91 |
| Kraus, Henry C.—1714 Paul Murphy, New Orleans, La. | | 77 |
| Kraus, Jerry—9 Grandview, Buffalo, N. J. | | 90 |
| Kresin, Marion—3241 W. Thomas, Chicago, Ill. | | 61 |
| Kriebs, Helen—Galena, Ill. | | 90 |
| Kriefall, Harold A.—811 Weed, Shawano, Wis. | | 24 |
| Krum, Edward L.—432 Elms, Lawrence, Kan. | | 48 |
| Kruse, Otto C., Jr.—Manning, Iowa. | | 32 |
| Krush, Henry B.—115-57 155th, Jamaica, L. I., N. Y. | | 93 |
| Kubin, Edward W.—Bryan, Tex. | | 21 |
| Kunish, Lester L.—12 E. Park, Randolph Field, Tex. | | 24 |
| Kurlat, Morris—Saluda, S. C. | | 66 |
| Kurtz, Myers R.—4815 Centre, Pittsburgh, Pa. | | 93 |
| Kuthan, Charles F.—Omaha, Neb. | | 17 |

### L

| | | |
|---|---|---|
| Lacy, Joe—Columbus, Miss. | | 26 |
| Lacroix, Albert A.—156 Mitchel, New Haven, Conn. | | 76 |
| LeFlure, Joseph E.—Riverside, Chestertown, N. Y. | | 26 |
| Lagace, Zeno E.—RFD 3, Winsted, Conn. | | 92 |
| Lake, J. E.—4351 Dickason, Dallas, Tex. | | 60 |
| Laing, Adelbert L.—Lubbock, Tex. | | 27 |
| Lamb, Myron—101 Shields, Youngstown, Ohio. | | 92 |
| Lancaster, Eugene B.—2617 N. 6th, Harrisburg, Pa. | | 101 |
| Landon, T. H.—Quarters 15, Army War Col., Washington, D. C. | 15, 91, 97 and | 20, 99 |
| Lane, David A.—Louisville, Ky. | | 11 |
| Lane, Joseph L.—St. Louis, Mo. | | 87 |
| Lang, Matthew—Rt. 2, Box 328, Amelia, Ohio. | | 11 |
| Larsen, Gordon O.—841-71st, Brooklyn, N. Y. | | 77 |
| Larson, Albert B.—Strattonville, Pa. | | 106 |
| Larson, Jerrold E.—Aitken, Minn. | | 27 |
| Larson, Roy O.—Bayou Chene, La. | | 26 |
| Lau, Eldo—103 E. Green Bay, Shawano, Wis. | | 83 |
| Laurendeau, Alfred P.—41 Alton, Somerville, Mass. | | 77 |
| Laverghetta, Nick—358 East, Dedham, Mass. | | 61 |
| Lawrence, Gertrude | | 62 |
| Lawrey, Daniel D.—2343 Clifton, Chicago, Ill. | | 21 |
| Lear, Fay F.—815 Waukesha, Butte, Mont. | | 101 |
| LeBlanc, Elliott J.—901-7th, Port Arthur, Tex. | | 46 |
| Ledbetter, J. E.—Rt. 1, Canton, Tex. | | 60 |
| Lee, Bob—5549 Delancy, Philadelphia, Pa. | | 91 |
| Lee, Cloy, L B.—136 S. Coats, Daytona Beach, Fla. | | 64 |
| Lee, Tonie—Box 103, Dallas Co., Wilmer, Tex. | | 76 |
| Lee, William F.—11158 Chandler, N. Hollywood, Calif. | | 33 |
| Legett, George—55 Kimball, Yonkers, N. Y. | | 46 |
| Leighton, James W.—1923 W. Fourth, Davenport, Iowa. | | 80 |
| Lejarre,, Louis J.—46 Romaine, Jersey City, N. J. | | 24 |
| Leof, Charles—4803-7th, Kenosha, Wis. | | 26 |
| Leonard, Henry—161 S. Sycamore, Los Angeles, Calif. | 18 and | 99 |
| Lester, Adolphus Y.—1726 Oakview, Decatur, Ga. | | 14 |
| Lester, Raymond N.—402 E. King, Quincy, Fla. | | 27 |
| Leventry, Robert R.—Johnstown, Pa. | | 70 |
| Levine, Leo A.—5819 Texas, Houston, Tex. | | 21 |
| Levit, Harold A.—51 Buchanan, Bronx, N. Y. | | 92 |
| Lewis, David M., Jr.—Woodstown, N. J. | | 36 |
| Leypold, John C.—724 Penn, Johnsonberg, Pa. | | 34 |
| Lieb, John, Jr.—Box 66, Atkins, Iowa. | | 20 |
| Liebgott, Edward—Box 248, Hill Field, Ogden, Utah. | | 93 |
| Lima, Edward—3629 Chestnut, Fort Wayne, Ind. | | 83 |
| Lippert, Walter L.—Burlington, Iowa. | | 67 |
| Lipscomb, D. H.—Box 933, Morgantown, W. Va. | | 91 |
| Loflin, William A.—908 W. 24th, Little Rock, Ark. | | 25 |
| Logan, James C.—119 W. Magnolia, San Antonio, Tex. | | 72 |
| Lomax, J. W.—1518 Pleaston, San Antonio, Texas. | | 61 |
| Lombardi, Eugene P.—135 Orchard, Penn Twsp. Wilkinsburg, Pa. | | 91 |

| NAME | ADDRESS | PAGE |
|---|---|---|
| Lombardi, Herman | | 95 |
| Long, E. E.—302 E. Plum, Robinson, Ill. | | 63 |
| Long, James E.—810 S. University, Knoxville, Tenn. | | 95 |
| Long, Walter B., Jr.—2749 Ordway, NW, Washington, D. C. | | 91 |
| Lowe, David S. | | 63 |
| Loyd, Eugene V.—1717-14th, So., Birmingham, Ala. | | 63 |
| Lubanski, Theodore V.—4540 S. Sacramento, Chicago, Ill. | | 31 and 77 |
| Lucas, John V.—Crawford, Neb. | | 76 |
| Lucas, Patricia—Honolulu, T. H. | | 11 |
| Ludemann, Frederick C.—177 Grand, White Plains, N. Y. | | 66 |
| Ludka, Arthur P.—3043 S. Lincoln, Englewood, Colo. | | 34 |
| Lukehart, Melvin L.—Mampa, Idaho | | 45 |
| Lustic, Stanley J.—Box 3, Elbert, W. Va. | | 39 |

### M

| NAME | ADDRESS | PAGE |
|---|---|---|
| MacInnis, John L.—Box 537, Edmond, Wash. | | 20 |
| MacPherson, Donald J.—Old Town, Me. | | 11 |
| Mahaffy, George B.—14860 Stakelin, Detroit, Mich. | | 69 |
| Maher, Phillip J.—7814-84th, Brooklyn, N. Y. | | 101 |
| Malene, Joseph C.—1113-13th, Tuskaloosa, Ala. | | 93 |
| Malley, T. F.—21 Linden, Brookline, Mass. | | 61 |
| Mallin, Robert I.—808 W. 67th, Kansas City, Mo. | | 93 |
| Malloy, Fran—Galveston, Jamaica Plain, Mass. | | 25 |
| Maltby, Albert E.—Box 346, Hastings, Fla. | | 63 |
| Mandt, H.—Richmond Hill, N. Y. | | 31 |
| Mangieri, Frank—309 E. Martin, Avington, Ill. | | 24 |
| Manning, Anne—508 Fifth, New Cumberland, Pa. | | 32 |
| Marsden, Roy F.—556 AAF BU, Long Beach, Calif. | | 65 |
| Martin, Charles A.—805 Traffic, Bossier City, La. | | 46 |
| Martin, Francis H.—211 W. Coal, Gallup, N. M. | | 11 |
| Martin, Fred K.—1025 Tenn, Ft. Wayne, Ind. | | 24 |
| Martin, George J.—496 Hickory, Arlington, N. J. | | 92 |
| Martin, John A.—527½ SW St., Bellevue, Ohio | | 36 |
| Martin, Neil T.—South Lincoln, Mass. | | 31 and 82 |
| Martin, Richard—Mishawaka, Ind. | | 29 |
| Marx, Harry K.—25 W. 16th, Indianapolis, Ind. | | 42 |
| Masczuk, Joseph P.—914 S. Prospect, Nanticoke, Pa. | | 102 |
| Mason, George R.—62nd AF BU (S&R) McChord Fld., Tacoma, Wash. | | 33 |
| | | 46 |
| Mason, John D.—1 W. Hillside, Lordship, Stratford, Conn. | | 36 |
| Matson, C. A.—1167 N. Curson, Hollywood, Calif. | | 46 |
| Mattison, Keith W.—22 Pine Port, Allegheny, Pa. | | 102 |
| Mattson, Conrad E.—1106 S. Michigan, Stevens Point, Wis. | | 101 |
| Mausling, William, Jr.—RFD No. 1, Thompson, Ohio | | 31 |
| Mays, John L.—700 W. Haymond, Shelbyville, Ind. | | 25 |
| Meagher, Richard J.—229 E. 201st, New York, N. Y. | | 91 |
| Meehan, Edward—12 Ash, Woburn, Mass. | | 75 |
| Meeker, Albert—156 Fair, Patterson, N. J. | | 31 |
| Megraw, Arthur J.—917 Lincoln, Prospect Park, Pa. | | 67 |
| Mehaffey, Nathan G.—Gorman, Tex. | | 26 and 27 |
| Meiborg, Robert W.—640 Fairfield, Elmhurst, Ill. | | 92 |
| Mellas, Lawrence L.—420 Main, Edwardsville, Pa. | | 15 |
| Meng, James M.—4425 Normand, Ft. Worth, Tex. | | 24 |
| Menzer, Harry—Pittsburgh, Pa. | | 11 |
| Merrifield, Harry B.—1210 Porter Bldg., Portland, Ore. | | 32 |
| Merritt, Jack—Saranac Lake, N. Y. | | 21 |
| Metcalf, George N.—206 W. Franklin, Wheaton, Ill. | | 90 |
| Mettes, Lloyd Q.—Atlanta, Mo. | | 48 |
| Michel, Richard P.—464 N. Race, Springfield, Ohio | | 66 |
| Middaugh, Vance—428 Casa Loma, Bakersfield, Calif. | | 103 |
| Mikesell, Ralph O.—2020-8th, SE, Cedar Rapids, Iowa | | 61 |
| Milam, Robert A.—2715 Pittsburg, Houston, Texas | | 25 |
| Miller, Charles B. | | 63 |
| Miller, E. B., Jr.—Viola, Kan. | | 98 |
| Miller, Keith H.—Enterprise, Ore. | | 32 |
| Miller, Robert C.—541½ W. Clinton, Frankfort, Ind. | | 11 |
| Millin, Fred R.—230 Vernon, Norwood, Mass. | | 66 |
| Mills, Daniel W.—50 Mt. Vernon, Frederickstown, Ohio | | 61 |
| Mills, Leonard L.—RFD 2, Gates, Tenn. | | 60 |
| Minsker, John E.—236 S. Coronada, Apt. 310 Los Angeles, Calif. | | 33 |
| Misick, Arnold C.—Coaldale, W. Va. | | 21 |
| Mitchell, John W.—OMR Box 85, Keesler Fld., Miss. | | 92 and 101 |
| Mitchell, Jule C., Jr.—RFD, Pittsview, Ala. | | 102 |
| Modelski, Edward V.—106 Hearthcote, Elmont, L. I., N. Y. | | 77 |
| Mollenkope, Earl R.—343 Winckles, Elyria, Ohio | | 95 |
| Moloznick, Peter—Chicago, Ill. | | 33 |
| Monday, William D—282 Willow, Mt. Airy, N. C. | | 90 |
| Mondro, Edward J.—1253 N. Campbell, Chicago, Ill. | | 101 |
| Moner, Michael | | 95 |
| Montgomery, Charles—Rt. 3, Deleware, Okla. | | 67 |
| Moore, Douglas B.—119 S. Jarrot, Florence, S. C. | | 101 |
| Moore, Ernest M.—HQ 4th AF, Hamilton Field, Calif. | | 97 and 101 |
| Moore, Jean—470 Arlington, Elgin, Ill. | | 92 |
| Moore, Ralph—Saline, La. | | 67 |
| Moore, Robert W.—Anchorage, Ky. | | 101 |
| Moore, Wallace C.—801 Cabanus, Edenton, N. C. | | 15 |
| Moore, Wilbert C.—3503 Barret, Lemay, Mo. | | 18 and 21 |
| Moos, Louis—844 Second East, Kallspell, Mont. | | 20 |
| Morehart, Clifton E.—Tulsa, Okla. | | 15 |
| Moreland, John H.—Woodbury, La. | | 25 |
| Morgan, Frances—2908 Fitzhugh, Dallas, Tex. | | 64 and 65 |
| Morgan, Jack W.—25 Wilma, Youngstown, Ohio | | 91 |
| Morgan, John P.—Baecon, Mattapoisett, Mass. | | 32 |
| Morgan, Joseph F.—58 Main, Nicholas, N. Y. | | 25 |
| Morlock, William J.—4 Alma, Buffalo, N. Y. | | 36 |
| Morris, Emil, Jr.—1701 S. Montgomery, Sedalia, Mo. | | 31 |
| Morrison, Howard A.—1313 S. Broadway, Albert Lea, Minn. | | 84 |
| Morrison, James B.—Orano, Me. | | 75 |
| Morrison, Robert D.—11 Holland Apts., Havre, Mont. | | 75 |
| Morrow, John J.—Greensboro, N. C. | | 97 |
| Morrow, W. P. | | 63 |
| Moseley, T. E.—Westwood, Mass. | | 67 |
| Moss, Harold A.—4237 Oakland, Minneapolis, Minn. | | 24 |
| Moss, O. V.—3539 N. Littlejohn, Ft. Worth, Tex. | | 60 |
| Motley, Jack—Rt. 4, Dallas, Tex. | | 60 |
| Mott, Bernard—Galesburg, Ill. | | 32 |
| Mueller, Alex—1420 Ontario, Sheboygan, Wis. | | 95 |

| NAME | ADDRESS | PAGE |
|---|---|---|
| Mueller, Fred E., Jr.—117 Lilac La., San Antonio, Tex. | | 29 |
| Mullens, Marshall E.—Omaha, Neb. | | 48 |
| Murphy, Fred E., Jr.—Macon, Ga. | | 37 |
| Murphy, James—535 Mount Calm, St. Paul, Minn. | | 36 |
| Murphy, Raymond—Appalachia, Va. | | 24 |
| Murray, Forrest J.—Lu AAF, Box 124, Las Vegas, Nev. | | 93 |
| Musgrave, Charles L.—1155 Sherman, Denver, Colo. | | 107 |
| Myers, Leroy A.—1021 Beaumont, Port Arthur, Tex. | | 92 |
| Myers, William B.—556 Bradley, Columbus, Ohio | | 61 and 77 |
| McAllister, Virginia—701 Hillcrest, Moultrie, Ga. | | 65 |
| McCain, Thomas R.—Baton Rouge, La. | | 68 |
| McCain, Vice Adm. | | 97 |
| McCallum, Reavis H.—1108 College, Indianapolis, Ind. | | 102 |
| McCandless, Joseph A.—239 Fourth, Ellwood City, Pa. | | 27 |
| McCardy, Monty G., Jr.—Box 32, Stanford, Mont. | | 20 |
| McCarthy, Pat B.—1034 Harrison, Defiance, Ohio | | 23 |
| McConnell, John—27 Center, Morristown, N. J. | | 85 |
| McCorkle, Quentin—Nimrod, Ky. | | 101 |
| McCormic, Joseph A., Jr.—101 S. Fairview, Upper Darby, Pa. | | 102 |
| McCormick, Richard E., Jr.—2808 Corning, Parsons, Kan. | | 31 |
| McCorrisoon, Mrs. Robt.—Honolulu, T. H. | | 11 |
| McCourry, Ray—13 Grace, Morrison Homes, W. Palm Beach, Fla. | | 33 |
| McCoy, Henry E.—1716 Main, Sisterville, W. Va. | | 17 |
| McCue, Marcello | | 29 |
| McCumber, Myrle W.—2131 Hagerman, Colo. Springs, Colo. | | 101 |
| McCune, Harvey G.—515 Iolani Ave., Honolulu, T. H. | | 21 |
| McCurdy, Richard L.—Riverside, Augusta, Me. | | 24 |
| McDonald, Orville—1501 8th, Lawrenceville, Ill. | | 83 |
| McElligott, William T.—Chicago, Ill. | | 11 |
| McGlothlin, Carlton—Hardy, Va. | | 33 |
| McGowan, Tom—Box 21-A, Rt. 2, Warren, Tex. | | 11 |
| McHam, Charles W.—633 N. Penn, Indianapolis, Ind. | | 63 |
| McIlvaine, Alexander W.—121 LeMoyne, Washington, Pa. | | 20 |
| McIlvaine, John W.—150 Wilmont, Washington, Pa. | | 92 |
| McIntosh, Claude—625 Wildwood, Columbia, S. C. | | 67 |
| McKenna, Bernard J.—57 Tarleton, Oakwood Beach, L. I., N. Y. | | 14 |
| McKinney, Homer—Atlanta, Ga. | | 91 |
| McLaughlin, James B.—112 E. 1st, Oil City, Pa. | | 69 |
| McLellan, Albert H.—102 Yates, Macon, Ga. | | 68 |
| McNaughton, Kenneth P. | | 96 |
| McShane, Girlie—Honolulu, T. H. | | 11 |

### N

| NAME | ADDRESS | PAGE |
|---|---|---|
| Nagel, Don O.—RR 1, New Weston, Ohio | | 63 |
| Nagy, John A.—Carmichaels, Pa. | | 68 |
| Napolitano, August A.—519 Benson, Camden, N. J. | | 77 |
| Nason, Donald A.—RFD No. 3, Gardiner, Me. | | 99 |
| Naylor, Leon J.—Troy, N. J. | | 36 |
| Neal, Mary—1847 Charles, E. Cleveland, Ohio | | 64 |
| Nelson, Kenneth R.—Lake, Brockport, N. Y. | | 66 |
| Neresian, John—710 S. Cotterell, Detroit, Mich. | | 90 |
| Nesley, W. L.—909 Rolla, Rolla, Mo. | | 24 |
| Neulreigh, Robert J.—2121 S. 79th, West Allis, Wis. | | 26 |
| Neuroth, Roscoe C.—Fennimore, Wis. | | 77 |
| Newhouse, Charles H.—2415 Amherst, Des Moines, Iowa | | 90 |
| Nicholas, George P.—3219 Fourth, Sacramento, Calif. | | 33 |
| Nicholson, William A.—Escanaba, Mich. | | 87 |
| Nicholson, W. H. 911 Park, McKeesport, Pa. | | 67 |
| Nieman, Robert A.—3243 Daytona, Cincinnati, Ohio | | 91 |
| Niemi, William J.—1215 Eighth, Anchorage, Alaska | | 25 and 33 |
| Nims, Jay R.—Staples, Minn. | | 62 |
| Noble, Dale—2510 Dodier, St. Louis, Mo. | | 11 |
| Nocher, C. A.—123 Greenwich, Pittsfield, Mass. | | 61 |
| Nolte, Ursel C.—7309 McKinley, Los Angeles, Calif. | | 46 |
| Norton, Thomas—Dorchester, Mass. | | 12 and 67 |

### O

| NAME | ADDRESS | PAGE |
|---|---|---|
| Obenshain, Ray L., Jr.—626 Princetown, Fresno, Calif. | | 103 |
| O'Connor, Thomas F.—8 Pattison, Worcester, Mass. | | 25 |
| Odoleski, Bernard R. | | 63 |
| O'Donnel, Burton—Box 774, Chelan, Wash. | | 70 |
| Odom, Otis, Jr.—Rt. 1, Stanton, Tex. | | 100 |
| Ogus, Allen G.—700-A 9th, NW, Washington, D. C. | | 20 |
| Ogus, Bert—3757 W. Arlington, Chicago, Ill. | | 21 |
| O'Hara, James P. | | 63 |
| O'Hara, Robert C.—Louisville, Ky. | | 27 |
| O'Hara, Robert G.—514 Aberdeen, Dayton, Ohio | | 25 and 102 |
| O'Hare, John M.—2614 Elm, River Grove, Ill. | | 24 |
| Olds, Arthur—142 Washington, Hartford, Mich. | | 36 |
| Olds, Harry—345 Beldon, Chicago, Ill. | | 21 |
| Olin, Edmond J. | | 63 |
| Oliver, John H., Jr.—205 W. Church, Edenton, N. C. | | 90 |
| Olysav, John F.—Box 295, Terrace, Pa. | | 87 |
| O'Neil, Jim—Jamaica, L. I., N. Y. | | 24 |
| Opperman, Conrad—3633 Russell, St. Louis, Mo. | | 14 |
| Orbon, Thomas F.—540 Union, Hudson, N. Y. | | 92 |
| Orme, Frank—1840 Biltmore, Washington, D. C. | | 93 |
| O'Rourke, (Davenport) Dorothy M.—809 E. Walnut, Harrisburg, Ill. | | 24, 64 and 65 |
| Oswell, Clyde W.—Box 1108, Ely, Nev. | | 92 |
| Otto, William K.—27 Maple, Dexter, Me. | | 31 |
| Oyler, Kenneth D.—Box 25, Burlington, Ind. | | 24 and 25 |

### P

| NAME | ADDRESS | PAGE |
|---|---|---|
| Pack, Karl A.—6914 Franklin, Hollywood, Calif. | | 102 |
| Page, Thomas G.—3205 Arctic, Atlantic, N. J. | | 42 |
| Pahl, Elmer T.—216 Vine, Lodi, Calif. | | 26 |
| Panyard, A. K.—7426 Churchill, Detroit, Mich. | | 60 |
| Park, C. A.—308 SE Levee, Brownsville, Tex. | | 60 |
| Park, Winston, H.—1107 Ave., "A", Flint, Mich. | | 25 |
| Parker, G. W.—2437 Pine Lake, Keego Harbor, Mich. | | 61 |
| Parker, James | | 96 |
| Parker, L. L.—5611 Winslow, Dallas, Tex. | | 60 |
| Parker, William E.—5835 Shattuck, Oakland, Calif. | | 29 |
| Parker, William T.—2718 S. Cleveland, Philadelphia, Pa. | | 14 |
| Parrott, Harold—Salt Lake City, Utah | | 90 |
| Pasqua, Joseph—3314 White Plains, Bronx, N. Y. | | 77 |

| NAME | ADDRESS | PAGE |
|---|---|---|
| Pate, Garland H.—Rt. 3, Hanceville, Ala. | | 66 |
| Pato, Wilhelm | | 63 |
| Patrick, Andrew—27E N. Hany, State College, Pa. | | 24 |
| Patrick, T. A.—3863 Gladwin, Detroit, Mich. | 60 and | 61 |
| Patterson, Nolan D.—2136 Fairview, Wichita, Kan. | | 31 |
| Paul Harold C.—440 Calvin, Buffalo, N. Y. | 11 and | 15 |
| Paul, William V.—4761 Oak, Merchantville, N. J. | | 25 |
| Paullin, David W.—Rt. 1, Brookville, Ohio. | | 63 |
| Pavesick, John—319 Hayes, McDonald, Ohio. | | 94 |
| Paxton, John W.—HQ AAF, Office of Air Eng., Washington, D. C. | | 92 |
| Payne, Joseph—Fort Shoals, Greenville, Tenn. | | 37 |
| Pearce, Andrew W.—Rt. 1, South Mills, N. C. | | 26 |
| Pearson, Robert B.—RFD, Markhan, Va. | 18 and | 21 |
| Pecorari, Frank V.—440 Kearny, Kearny, N. J. | | 11 |
| Peiffer, Richard D.—501 S. Main, Mishawaka, Ind. | | 39 |
| Pelfrey, Andrew—325 E. Walnut. Apt. 8, Indianapolis, Ind. | | 11 |
| Pennington, L. E.—Box 374, Pontiac, Mich. | | 61 |
| Penrose, Julian—Plymouth Meeting, Pa. | | 29 |
| Pentek, William H.—2 Va, Huntington, L. I., N. Y. | | 15 |
| Perkins, Claud D.—Livingston, Tex. | | 70 |
| Perkins, R.—3505 Hurlbut, Detroit, Mich. | | 60 |
| Perontoni, Jose M.—Barke, N. Cannaan, Litchfield, Conn. | | 99 |
| Perry, George E.—1353 1 Washburn, Detroit, Mich. | | 105 |
| Perry, Henry—Raritan, Ill. | | 92 |
| Perry, William E.—2747 Preece, San Diego, Calif. | | 14 |
| Perryman, Albert H.—717 S. 23rd, Ft. Smith, Ark. | | 20 |
| Petersham, Miska, F.—Woodstock, N. Y. | | 25 |
| Peterson, C. D., Jr.—Rt. 3, Merkel, Tex. | | 83 |
| Peterson, Dale—Boy River, Minn. | | 61 |
| Peyton, D. T.—Charleston, Mo. | | 24 |
| Phillips, George D.—New Rochelle, N. Y. | | 36 |
| Phillips, Hilton—Eros, La. | | 81 |
| Phillips, Willard—506 N. Congress, Rushville, Ill. | | 32 |
| Phinney, Donald E.—20 E. 11th, Columbus, Ohio. | | 61 |
| Pierce, Elton—Rt. 2, Lucedale, Miss. | | 101 |
| Pieri, Mario W.—1445 Stockton, San Francisco, Calif. | | 83 |
| Pike, Warren R.—6915 S. Sangamon, Chicago, Ill. | 24 and | 85 |
| Pinn, Charles H.—Ottawa, Ill. | | 77 |
| Piper, John A. | | 101 |
| Pirch, Frank—4308 Kenmore, Chicago, Ill. | | 61 |
| Pittman, Eugene R.—4511 N. Haven, Toledo, Ohio. | | 26 |
| Pluskwik, Donald S.—830-15th, N. Virginia, Minn. | | 29 |
| Pollard, Harold W.—831 Fortuna, Calif. | | 92 |
| Polzin, Charles A., Jr.—3245 S. 25th, Milwaukee, Wis. | | 36 |
| Poole, Raymond C. | | 34 |
| Poorman, Albert D.—West Union, Ill. | | 66 |
| Porter, Dale L.—Steadman, Nome, Alaska. | | 33 |
| Porter, Floy—Memphis, Tenn. | | 48 |
| Porter, James S.—Toledo, Ore. | | 45 |
| Postle, Edgar W.—Rt. 5, Hillsboro, Ohio. | | 21 |
| Powell, Walter M.—2211 Orcutt, Newport News, Va. | | 102 |
| Power, M. A.—3443 Sutherland, Indianapolis, Ind. | | 61 |
| Powers, C. L.—843-21st, Santa Monica, Calif. | | 61 |
| Preston, William J.—Box 218, E. Brady, Pa. | 33 and | 34 |
| Price, Richard L.—W. 1833 Mollon, Apt. D, Spokane, Wash. | | 82 |
| Priest Loran R.—Rt. 3, Sabetha, Kan. | | 29 |
| Pruitt, Tommy—Rt. 1, Ringling, Okla. | | 76 |
| Pukas, Elizabeth—515 W. 168th, New York, N. Y. | 64 and | 65 |

**Q**

| NAME | ADDRESS | PAGE |
|---|---|---|
| Quinlan, Raymond F.—Pesotum, Ill. | | 27 |
| Quinn, Aldy B.—6946 Kernel, Houston, Tex. | | 62 |
| Quinn, Edward J.—Preston, Ill. | | 76 |
| Quinn, Francis P.—837 N. Montello, Brockton, Mass. | | 46 |

**R**

| NAME | ADDRESS | PAGE |
|---|---|---|
| Rabogliatti, Alfred—Globe, Ariz. | | 27 |
| Rainbolt, Lloyd J.—West Eminence, Mo. | | 42 |
| Rainey, James E.—251 Forrest, Ambler, Pa. | | 63 |
| Rainwater, Charles O.—704 3rd SW, Moultrie, Ga. | | 103 |
| Ransburg, George D.—Pleasant Lake, Ind. | | 67 |
| Raphael, Eugene F.—403 Central, Towson, Md. | | 58 |
| Rasco, James J. | | 63 |
| Rasmussen, Jack F.—2700 Eldridge, Bellingham, Wash. | | 101 |
| Rawlings, William M.—Onawa, Iowa. | | 93 |
| Readinger, Calvin L.—47 N. 4th, Reading, Pa. | | 66 |
| Reardon, Mary—217 Sargeant, Hartford, Conn. | | 64 |
| Rearick, Chester—Martinsburg, Pa. | | 90 |
| Reasoner, Douglas B.—Mine, Flemington, N. J. | | 33 |
| Reckard, John—62 W. Church, Fairchance, Pa. | | 21 |
| Redfield, Robert W.—314 Ave. "C", Cloquet, Minn. | | 101 |
| Redick, Kenneth L.—31 Carney, Tonawanda, N. Y. | | 20 |
| Reece, Clifford—1585 S. St. Paul, Denver, Colo. | | 33 |
| Reed, Warren G., Jr.—3209 Ivanhoe, Baton Rouge, La. | | 102 |
| Reen, Victor A.—RR L, Crows Landing, Calif. | | 25 |
| Reese, Vernon. | | 63 |
| Reeve, Margaret—508 Blvd. Heights, Calhoun, Ga. | | 65 |
| Reeves, Russell E., Jr.—Memphis, Tenn. | | 108 |
| Refermat, Richard S.—1394 Electric, Lackawanna, N. Y. | | 32 |
| Reiber, Ray R.—1225 Atwood, Akron, Ohio. | | 62 |
| Reid, Arthur—202 Martin, East Point, Ga. | | 32 |
| Reitz, William H.—3308 N. Sacramento, Chicago, Ill. | | 90 |
| Renner, George—2309 Lillie, Ft. Wayne, Ind. | | 25 |
| Rettberg, Gebhard C.—306 E. Green, Champaigne, Ill. | | 102 |
| Retzlaff, Leon F.—Wonewoc, Wis. | 32 and | 77 |
| Rhode, John A.—Clovis, Calif. | | 26 |
| Riave, Lionel, L.—Box 146, Carmarillo, Calif. | | 27 |
| Rice, William E.—2510 N. Dewey, Oklahoma City, Okla. | | 66 |
| Richards, Merl—Granite Falls, Wash. | | 20 |
| Richardson, Robert C., Jr. | 95 and | 97 |
| Richardson, Virgil A.—404 E. Fourth, Spencerville, Ohio. | | 77 |
| Richins, Joseph G.—11C St., Brookside Park, Springville, Utah. | | 101 |
| Riggs, John A.—516 E. Taylor, Reno, Nev. | | 31 |
| Rigney, Dale—25 Lexington, NW, Grand Rapids, Mich. | | 85 |
| Riley, Gerald E.—2409 S. Clinton, Sioux City, Iowa. | | 26 |
| Rini, Thomas M., Jr.—3633 Reidham, Shaker Heights, Ohio. | | 31 |
| Rippetoe, Robert M.—Wichita, Kans. | | 67 |
| Riston, Alvin G.—Green Bay, Wis. | | 20 |
| Ritter, Ivan—203 West Williams, Greenville, Mich. | | 29 |
| Roark, Jacob—Wyoming, Ill. | | 93 |
| Robbins, Ted E.—605 W. Main, Bloomsburg, Pa. | | 11 |
| Roberts, Alvin E., Jr.—914 E. 6th, Tucson, Ariz. | | 101 |
| Roberts, Carson—Coronado, Calif. | | 24 |
| Roberts, Walter N.—1608 Harlem, Rockford, Ill. | | 102 |
| Robinson, Herbert D.—18913 Cherokee, Cleveland, Ohio. | | 91 |
| Robinson, Moses—Rt. 1, Box 1, Camden, S. C. | | 85 |
| Robinson, Paul C.—Rt. 1, Wellington, Kan. | | 45 |
| Rockwell, Robert—RFD No. 1, Troy, N. Y. | | 21 |
| Rode, Erwin A.—211 S. Old, Tulare, Mass. | | 32 |
| Roepke, D. E.—3956 Boulevard Pl., Indianapolis, Ind. | | 61 |
| Rogus, T. J.—4748 Melville, E. Chicago, Ind. | | 61 |
| Rohmer, Frank—65 Mt. Vernon, Needham, Mass. | | 12 |
| Romer, Reginald P.—1547 W. Myrtle, Seattle, Wash. | | 36 |
| Rongstad, Wallace—Box 66, Kalispell, Mont. | 26 and | 83 |
| Rookstool, W. D.—847 NE 20th, Oklahoma City, Okla. | | 67 |
| Ross, Robert H., Jr.—Dayton Pike, Germantown, Ohio. | | 24 |
| Rothrock, C. W.—Webster City, Iowa. | | 61 |
| Rott, T/5—1749 N. Honore, Chicago, Ill. | | 61 |
| Roush, Irvin N.—417 Front, N. Umberland, Pa. | | 84 |
| Rowe, John F.—235 Emmett St., Virden, Ill. | | 36 |
| Rozell, Leland E.—1801 Roosevelt, Houston, Tex. | | 83 |
| Rubin, Kenneth S.—149 S. Alta Vista, Los Angeles, Calif. | | 77 |
| Rudolph Walter A.—210-02 Nashville, St. Albans, L. I., N. Y. | | 35 |
| Russell, Howard E.—197 Fairfield, Hartford, Conn. | | 93 |
| Russell, H. W.—831 Bradley, Chicago, Ill. | | 61 |
| Russell, Paul E.—206 Holmes, Indianapolis, Ind. | | 11 |
| Rutledge, Jay—Ind Coll Armed Forces, Rm 1E585 Pentagon, Washington, D. C. | 20 and | 21 |
| Ryan, Fred J., Jr.—34 North Dr., Malba, L. I., N. Y. | | 62 |
| Ryan, William O. | | 97 |
| Ryder, Lawrence M.—219 Federal, Portland, Me. | | 84 |
| Rynearson, Bert R.—Fairbanks, Alaska | | 33 |
| Rzehak, Horace F.—Peru, Neb. | | 24 |

**S**

| NAME | ADDRESS | PAGE |
|---|---|---|
| Sackowitz, Isadore—4 N Coop Circle, Roosevelt, N. J. | | 25 |
| Saddler, Edwin E.—1342 N. Capitol, Salem, Ore. | | 21 |
| Salemi, Matteo—81 Spring, Manville, R. I. | | 103 |
| Salzillo, Vince—577 Harris, Providence, R. I. | | 91 |
| Sanchez, Joseph V. | | 63 |
| Sanders, Henry G.—433-14th, NW, Atlanta, Ga. | 24, 90, 102 and | 103 |
| Sanders, Lewis M.—Air Com. SS, Maxwell Field, Ala. | 75 and | 97 |
| Santucci, Dominic—920 S. Ashland, Chicago, Ill. | | 24 |
| Sapio, Don—21 Elliott, East Orange, N. J. | | 25 |
| Sather, Francis B.—Anchorage, Alaska | | 33 |
| Sattler, A. P.—8031 Abington, Detroit, Mich. | | 60 |
| Satterfield, H. E.—1605 Ave. B., San Antonio, Tex. | | 61 |
| Saylor, Paul M. | | 63 |
| Scamara, Robert S.—340 Pismo, San Luis Obispo, Calif. | | 92 |
| Scanlon, M. F. | | 97 |
| Schaefer, Bernard J.—Rt. 4, Oakhill Gardens, N. Kansas City, Mo. | | 77 |
| Schaeffer, William H.—Richland Springs, Tex. | | 93 |
| Scharf, Adolph A.—422 N. Spaulding, Los Angeles, Calif. | | 33 |
| Schartz, Francis T.—1118 Mainden Lane, Springfield, Ohio. | | 63 |
| Schauer, Louis—201 Grand, Hartford, Wis. | | 21 |
| Scheidler, Howard R. | | 63 |
| Schell, James—407 E. Washington, Harvard, Ill. | | 33 |
| Schild, Marcus A.—1701 Wisconsin, New Holstein, Wis. | | 92 |
| Schilling, J. C.—6401 W. Park, St. Louis, Mo. | | 60 |
| Schimpf, Hector J. | | 63 |
| Schlewitt, Robert—2251 Sheffield, Chicago, Ill. | | 33 |
| Schliesman, Donald—1706 W. Riverside, Spokane, Wash. | | 35 |
| Schneckenburger, B.—Long Island, N. Y. | | 24 |
| Scholder, Jack—922 Greene, Brooklyn, N. Y. | | 32 |
| Scholl, Daniel D.—1844 Section, Cincinnati, Ohio. | | 91 |
| Schomber, John R.—1016 S. Church, Belleville, Ill. | | 99 |
| Schuh, Robert P.—1545 NW First, Miami, Fla. | | 102 |
| Schurr, Paul—431 N. Frances, Madison, Wis. | | 93 |
| Scollon, Kenneth M.—309 N. 15th, Barnesboro, Pa. | | 14 |
| Scott, James M.—1111 Vine, Brownwood, Tex. | | 21 |
| Scruggs, Riley R.—Apt. T-2, Bowdoin Cts., Brunswick, Me. | | 92 |
| Seaman, George M.—Torrington, Wyo. | | 21 |
| Sedillo, Bolislo—764 E. 10th, Los Angeles, Calif. | | 33 |
| Seidel, James A.—Redrock, Tex. | | 27 |
| Seiler, Donald J.—239 N. Firestone, Akron, Ohio. | | 92 |
| Sekerac, John M.—Rt. 1, Box 125A, Davis, Calif. | | 20 |
| Sellers, Louis J.—204-12th, Loraine, Ohio. | | 99 |
| Shaner, Roy C.—1447 Locust, Pasadena, Cal. | | 66 |
| Shank, Harold A.—Guernsey, Pa. | | 93 |
| Sharp, Joffree H.—Haw River, N. C. | 24, 25 and | 42 |
| Shaw, Asa H.—Hermiston, Ore. | | 75 |
| Shaw, Guy L.—Box 476, Grants Pass, Ore. | | 21 |
| Shelhamer, Ellis—1881 S. St. Paul, Denver, Col. | 36, 90 and | 103 |
| Shelton, Fred B., Jr.—500 S. Marlborough, Dallas, Tex. | | 84 |
| Shelton, Hendricks L.—Danville Va. | | 21 |
| Sherer, Irwin—4719½ W. 28th, Los Angeles, Calif. | | 31 |
| Shields, Harland D.—Fairbanks, Alaska. | | 33 |
| Shields, Richard—1116-Eighth, Rockway, Pa. | | 84 |
| Shields, Robert B.—167 Arlington, Providence, R. I. | | 36 |
| Shiels, Thomas D.—1009 Comm. Standard Bldg. Fort Worth, Tex. | | 25 |
| Shinkowski, Charles L.—112 Willow Grove, Hackettstown, N. J. | | 26 |
| Shinsky, Alexander—Elyria, Ohio. | | 42 |
| Shirley, Fred A.—Clayton, Ala. | | 101 |
| Shoemaker, Jack E.—3417 NE 43rd, Portland, Ore. | | 24 |
| Shuman, Mary E.—1119 Sells, SW, Atlanta, Ga. | 64 and | 65 |
| Shumarsky, Philip—632 Garden, Hartford, Conn. | | 31 |
| Simoes, Joseph—755 Rodman, Fall River, Mass. | 67 and | 71 |
| Simpson, Russell A.—Seattle, Wash. | | 26 |
| Sims, Warren L.—930 B Ave., Coronado, Calif. | | 46 |
| Sinauer, Alan B.—4 Seymour, White Plains, N. Y. | | 24 |
| Sites, Herbert V.—5101 Webster, Apt. 10, W. Palm Beach, Fla. | | 21 |
| Sivik, Stanley A.—132 Baldwin, Bloomfield, N. J. | | 91 |
| Slater, J. W.—Hayt Corners, N. Y. | | 101 |
| Slattery, Joseph—55 Horadon, Roxbury, Mass. | | 25 |

| Name | Address | Page |
|---|---|---|
| Sloop, Robert, R. Rt. 2, Mooresville, N. C. | | 90 |
| Smith, Alfred—39 Park, Summerville, Mass. | | 33 |
| Smith, Earl L.—OMR, Box 483, Langley Field, Va. | | 92 |
| Smith, George H. | | 100 |
| Smith, George K.—26 St. John's Pl., Stamford, Conn. | | 25 |
| Smith, Glenn O.—Oxford Junction, Iowa | | 33 |
| Smith, Grover M.—4052 Pasadena, Seattle, Wash. | | 99 |
| Smith, J. E.—1018 S. Barr, Ft. Wayne, Ind. | | 11 |
| Smith, Joseph N.—Rt. 2, Box 71, Fort Pierce, Fla. | | 60 |
| Smith, J. O.—Birmingham, Ala. | | 67 |
| Smith, Julius E.—137 S. 10th, Pocatello, Idaho | | 102 |
| Smith, L. R.—612 14th, Antioch, Calif. | | 60 |
| Smith, Leroy C.—420 E. DeWald, Fort Wayne, Ind. | | 103 |
| Smith, M. W.—Fontanelle, Iowa | | 61 |
| Smith, S. L.—1213 Avalon, Waterloo, Iowa | | 61 |
| Smith, Thomas E.—1214-4th, SE, Minneapolis, Minn. | | 21 |
| Smith, William | | 33 |
| Sneed, Richard E.—511-1st, NW, Manden, N.D. | | 21 |
| Snellgrove, J. Frank—525 W. Matthews, Jonesboro, Ark. | | 45 |
| Sniezek, Harry—5896 Chopin, Detroit, Mich. | | 24 |
| Snipes, Gilmer L.—Seneca, S. C. | | 101 |
| Snook, Walter B.—Martin, Monterey, Calif. | | 32 |
| Snyder, James R.—New Cumberland, Pa. | | 102 |
| Snyder, James R.—Baltimore, Md. | | 92 and 93 |
| Sofio, Fred—505 E. Longyear, Bessemer, Mich. | | 39 |
| Sokol, Alex—10900 Olivet, Cleveland, Ohio | | 91 |
| Sommers, Walter A.—14425 Athens, Lakewood, Ohio | | 31 |
| Spain, DeWit—52 S. Hymes, Memphis, Tenn. | | 102 |
| Spano, Joseph T.—6325 S. Wolcott, Chicago, Ill. | | 74 |
| Sparkey, Otto—Box 13, Rice Lake, Wis. | | 85 |
| Spence, Kenneth G.—412 B No. Acacia, Compton, Calif. | | 21 |
| Spence, Thomas B.—Box 787, Salisbury, Md. | | 27 |
| Spense, Reginald O.—Farmington, Mo. | | 91 |
| Speshock, Leo E.—197 Pittsburgh, Uniontown, Pa. | | 38, 101 and 102 |
| Spitzer, Edward J.—18 Hillside, Teaneck, N. J. | | 21 |
| Spivey, J. T.—609 W. 38th, Norfolk, Va. | | 25 and 102 |
| Spoelker, Bernard A.—1226 W. Oak, Louisville, Ky. | | 67 |
| Spoerlein, LeRoy J.—734 N. Belmont, Arlington Hgts., Ill. | | 66 |
| Sprague, Melvin—191 Country, Tenafly, N. J. | | 35 |
| Sprung, Jack—1587 E. 19th, Brooklyn, N. Y. | | 66 |
| Stallings, Mary P.—1014-21st, Rock Island, Ill. | | 64 |
| Stampe, Henry M.—Ramona, S. D. | | 25 |
| Standifer, Hugh R.—Rt. 1, Box 55, Braxton, Miss. | | 66 |
| Standley, L. M.—3529 Bingham, St. Louis, Mo. | | 60 |
| Stankard, Edward—338-11th, Elyria, Ohio | | 21 |
| Stanko, P. J.—828 Distel, Detroit, Mich. | | 60 |
| Stanley, Spencer—Old Town, Maine | | 17 |
| Starrett, Robert J., Jr.—18 Haddon, Westmont, N. J. | | 32 |
| Staten, Robert E.—2146 Webb, Indianapolis, Ind. | | 11 |
| Stay, Jesse E.—Huntington Park, Calif. | | 91 |
| Steele, William S.—2302 Loban, Yakima, Wash. | | 93 |
| Steele, William T.—Miami Beach, Fla. | | 11 |
| Steines, V. W.—Rt. 1, Bellevue, Iowa | | 61 |
| Stepowski, Sylvester A.—6147 Marcus, Detroit, Mich. | | 76 |
| Stillwell, Joseph | | 66 |
| Stockdale, Julian L.—5715 S. Trumbull, Chicago, Ill. | | 91 |
| Stockley, Tom—41 Waverly, Brighton, Mass. | | 25 and 75 |
| Stoerrle, Joseph F.—4554 N. 18th, Philadelphia, Pa. | | 92 |
| Stolnaker, Charlie—Independence, Ore. | | 68 |
| Stone, Irene E.—2526 Lexington, Harrisburg, Pa. | | 64 and 65 |
| Stone, Leo—7135 Linsdale, Detroit, Mich. | | 83 |
| Stone, Robert J.—Garvin, Minn. | | 39 |
| Stoner, Robert J.—Tracy, Minn. | | 38 |
| Stoner, Robert O.—2 Argyle, Harrisburg, Pa. | | 12 |
| Stout, Jessie—7111 Corpus Christi, Houston, Tex. | | 95 |
| Streff, Bernard M.—Roscommon, Mich. | | 26 |
| Strolovitz, Max—2338-63rd, Brooklyn, N. Y. | | 99 |
| Strong, Robert L.—East Farms, Wash. | | 92 |
| Stuart, Alfred V.—3886-6th, Los Angeles, Calif. | | 93 |
| Stuckman, C. L.—29 Pine, Canton, N. Y. | | 67 |
| Studley, Joseph N.—262 Parkland, W. Lynn, Mass. | | 36 |
| Stumbrowski, Theodore J.—3330 Dudley, Baltimore, Md. | | 90 |
| Sturgevant, Ralph I.—615 Rose, Rocky Mt. N. C. | | 12 |
| Sturm, Ed.—Sacramento, Calif. | | 87 |
| Sturm, Norton L.—Chicago, Ill. | | 33 |
| Sullivan, Jack—135 Monroe, San Antonio, Tex. | | 15 |
| Sullivan, James F.—Chicago, Ill. | | 33 |
| Sullivan, Joseph G.—Washington, D. C. | | 39 |
| Suta, Nick H.—358 High, Aurora, Ill. | | 29 |
| Sutterlin, H. D.—Box B, Midway, Ky. | | 90 |
| Sutton, John E.—Rock Hill, S. C. | | 84 |
| Swanson, Paul H.—Lowes Creek, Eau Claire, Wis. | | 25 |
| Swearingen, Victor C.—5242 Grayton, Detroit, Mich. | | 105 |
| Sweeney, S. W.—Plymouth, Wis. | | 24 |
| Sweet, Charles—506 Jackson, W. Frankfort, Ill. | | 24 |
| Swick, Mike M.—796 Eureka, Windber, Pa. | | 24 |
| Swientochowski, Edward—3606 Spruce, Wilmington, Del. | | 90 |
| Swinyard, James G.—427 E. 13th, S., Salt Lake City, Utah | | 27 |

### T

| Name | Address | Page |
|---|---|---|
| Tabbert, Carl—6368 Michigan, Detroit, Mich. | | 76 |
| Tallichet, W. L. | | 63 |
| Tapp, James B.—TSEPS—4B HQ AMC, Wright Field, Dayton O. | | 101 |
| Tardio, Jose M.—Society of Jesus, Garapan | | 67 |
| Task, Earl R.—AAF Board, Orlando, Fla. | | 99 |
| Taylor, Charles E.—999 BU AAF Board, Orlando, Fla. | | 75, 93 and 103 |
| Taylor, Eugene—South Shore, Ky. | | 34 |
| Taylor, James B., Jr.—4446 NE Going, Portland, Ohio | | 91 |
| Taylor, John L.—225 Lena, Nokomis, Ill. | | 23 |
| Teeters, Daniel V.—3529½ Fletcher, Los Angeles, Calif. | | 24 |
| Telshaw, Ned T.—833 Park, Omaha, Neb. | | 46 |
| Tennant, Charles W.—2423 W. Olymic, Spokane, Wash. | | 101 |
| Terrell, LaVern R.—Box 112, 653 Weber, Santa Fe, N. M. | | 93 |
| Terronea, Leobardo J.—1104 W. 3rd, Ames, Iowa | | 34 |
| Thola, R. A.—Bellevue, Iowa | | 61 |
| Thomas, Ernest R.—1635-17th, San Francisco, Calif. | | 37 and 101 |
| Thomas, R. J.—1944 Tennessee, Vallejo, Calif. | | 24 |
| Thomas, Robert D.—McClure, Pa. | | 29 |
| Thomas, Woodrow—Summerville, W. Va. | | 36 |
| Thompson, John D—4320 Hargrave, Santa Rosa, Calif. | | 103 |
| Thune, Edward—1616 Midland, Syracuse, N. Y. | | 33 |
| Thurman, Earl J.—1923 Adkin, Salt Lake City, Utah | | 46 |
| Tilforth, Clarence W.—1845 W. Mulberry, Baltimore, Md. | | 34 and 76 |
| Tilison, John—40-8th, Hudson, N. Y. | | 90 |
| Tingle, Billy R.—1110 Illinois, Fairfield, Calif. | | 77 |
| Titus, Kenneth W.—Rt. 2, Norwich, N. Y. | | 102 |
| Titus, Porter H.—1217 Olive, Sanger, Calif. | | 67 |
| Tomasini, Raymond J.—Box 122, Southwick, Mass. | | 91 |
| Tonilas, Michael C.—8828 Longworth, Detroit, Mich. | | 105 |
| Toomey, John W.—Keeseville, N. Y. | | 26 |
| Toovey, Marvin W.—215 High, Box 53, Depue, Ill. | | 45 |
| Torsey, John H.—Sioux Falls, S. D. | | 107 |
| Touhey, Robert F.—60 Smith, Charleston, S. C. | | 93 |
| Towers, J. H. | | 96 |
| Townsend, James G.—N 5418 Ash, Spokane, Wash. | | 24 |
| Trautner, Donald W.—1209 N. Palmway, Lake Worth, Fla. | | 21 |
| Trautner, William—St. Louis, Mo. | | 24 |
| Treece, Clifford W.—1524 NW 47th, Oklahoma City, Okla. | | 75 |
| Trejo, William H.—Poughkeepsie, N. Y. | | 75 |
| Trocki, Frank—24 Garfield, Hyde Pk., Boston, Mass. | | 25 |
| Trotter, Joseph C.—Dacusville, S. C. | | 21 |
| Troutman, William—634 S. Spring, Los Angeles, Calif. | | 85 |
| Trumbour, George W.—198 Manning, Needham Hgts., Mass. | | 25 |
| Truscott, James C.—3909 E. Galer, Seattle, Wash. | | 11 and 15 |
| Try, John C.—3-9th, Burlington, N. J. | | 21 |
| Turner, Gerald E. | | 25 |
| Turner, William J.—427 W. 79th, Chicago, Ill. | | 32 |
| Turowski, Daniel—2908 N. Lawndale, Chicago, Ill. | | 46 |
| Tweet, Harold M.—Teller, Alaska | | 33 |
| Tyers, John B.—144 S. Oakhurst, Beverly Hills, Calif. | | 91 |

### U

| Name | Address | Page |
|---|---|---|
| Underwood, A. L.—Pardsville, Ky. | | 24 |
| Uretta, Lawrence—Farrell, Pa. | | 16 |

### V

| Name | Address | Page |
|---|---|---|
| Valentino, Edward—1248 W. Lexington, Chicago, Ill. | | 29 |
| Van de Hey, James M.—80-19th, Hermosa, Calif. | | 101 |
| Van Etten, Robert—Highland Mills, N. Y. | | 26 |
| Van Helmond, Harold—1528 N. Main, Racine, Wis. | | 29 |
| Vannoy, Wallace—Box 132, Clearmont, Wyo. | | 33 |
| Van Sicklen, Juliette S.—Mora, N. M. | | 64 |
| Vargas, T.—Ft. Morgan, Colo. | | 11 |
| Vargo, Edward J.—2006 Torbenson, Cleveland, Ohio | | 31 |
| Veatch, Bernard W.—610 Manor, Austin, Tex. | | 93 |
| Velivils, A. J.—Baltimore, Md. | | 90 |
| Vendola, Mike—4355 W. Potomac, Chicago, Ill. | | 61 |
| Veverka, Joseph F.—618 E. First, Mitchell, S. D. | | 92 |
| Vickery, Robert K., Jr.—1118 Oxford, Berkeley, Calif. | | 31 |
| Vickery, William W.—Valley Mills, Tex. | | 26 |
| Viken, Jack C.—Detroit Lakes, Minn. | | 21 |
| Villalon, Enrique—Brownsville, Tex. | | 76 |
| Vincent, Frederick—411 E. 12th, Flint, Mich. | | 93 |
| Visner, William K.—1344 Hartwick, Rochester, Mich. | | 61 |
| Vitkevic, John J.—Catlin, Ill. | | 67 |
| Vogelsberg, Roy C.—2219 Begole, Flint, Mich. | | 26 and 83 |
| Vogt, John E.—Box 143, Ducor, Calif. | | 101 |

### W

| Name | Address | Page |
|---|---|---|
| Waddell, James A. | | 63 |
| Wagner, W. E.—415-18th, Newark, N. J. | | 60 |
| Waldren, Clifford R.—43 Cartwright, Sidney, N. Y. | | 92 |
| Waldron, R. L.—295 Tappan, Brookline, Mass. | | 99 |
| Walk, John W.—2000 N. Summit, Decatur, Ill. | | 36 and 82 |
| Walker, A. M.—Rt. 3, Livingston, Tex. | | 60 |
| Walker, Delbert H.—Rt. 3, Box 498, Hanford, Calif. | | 66 |
| Walker, Francis—25 Newburg, Quincy, Mass. | | 76 |
| Wallace, Uriel—Olympia, Wash. | | 58 |
| Wallenberg, Ellis—Cloutierville, La. | | 101 |
| Wallis, John B.—Rt. 2, Deland, Fla. | | 21 |
| Walmer, Harry E.—8 Cypress, Middletown, Pa. | | 102 |
| Walsh, Joseph P.—1307 Section, Cincinnati, Ohio | | 91 |
| Walski, Joseph I.—2006 W. 21st, Chicago, Ill. | | 29 |
| Warner, Farlie W.—3108 Roxbury, Birmingham, Ala. | | 85 |
| Warren, Vernon B.—RFD 1, Cedar Spring, Mich. | | 108 |
| Warshovsky, Herbert—2001 Ave. P., Brooklyn, N. Y. | | 24 |
| Washington, John O.—4308 Versailles, Dallas, Tex. | | 60 |
| Wasson, Wilbur G.—520 Spring, Evansville, Ind. | | 66 |
| Waters, Charles L.—Springfield, Ky. | | 90 |
| Waters, George E.—Box 543, Newport, Wash. | | 11 |
| Watson, Howard W.—Memphis, Tenn. | | 24 |
| Watson, V. K.—5102 Norwood, Baltimore, Md. | | 36 |
| Watson, William H.—625 N. Augusta, Tyler, Tex. | | 106 |
| Watt, Donald—Box 453, Bloomingdale, N. J. | | 20 |
| Webb, James V.—485 Lee, SW, Apt. 8, Atlanta, Ga. | | 32 |
| Webster, John—Salt Lake City, Utah | | 16 |
| Weddington, Leonard D. | | 100 |
| Wehrheim, M. V.—Weber City, Iowa | | 61 |
| Weisz, George V.—79 Maddoc, Atlanta, Ga. | | 27 |
| Wells, Robert P. | | 63 |
| Wendt, Robert A.—2363-A N. 38th, Milwaukee, Wis. | | 27 |
| Wenzel, Paul R., Jr.—Box 161, Needville, Tex. | | 60 |
| Wermuth, Lawrence—2227 Date, Louisville, Ky. | | 29 |
| West, Joseph E.—564 Palmer, Youngstown, Ohio | | 32 |
| Whalen, Charles W.—59 Lexington, Belmont, Mass. | | 25 |
| Wheatley, Donald A.—1104 S. Madison, Jonesboro, Ark. | | 26 |
| Wheeler, Chester C.—Bethel, Me. | | 84 |
| Wheeler, Frank H., Jr.—RFD 2, Cleveland, Miss. | | 103 |
| White, A. | | 45 |
| White, Allen D.—Rt. 4, Box 68, Sebastopal, Calif. | | 32 |
| White, Clifford B.—San Antonio, Tex. | | 21 |
| White, Edward M.—1602 E. North, Jackson, Mich. | | 85 |
| White, Francis—Kingstree, S. C. | | 20 |

| NAME | ADDRESS | PAGE |
|---|---|---|
| White, Richard C.—Waukon, Iowa | | 92 |
| White, Wallace W.—Dallas, Tex. | | 11 |
| Whitehead, Joseph—403 W. 2nd, Leland, Mass. | | 24 |
| Whitney, Donal—Oswego, N. Y. | | 29 |
| Whittemore, Thomas B.—2116 Broadway, Paducah, Ky. | | 90 |
| Whitmam, Richard H.—Pittsburgh, Pa. | | 67 |
| Whyrick, Lloyd A.—Box 406, Milford, Neb. | | 26 |
| Wiederhoeft, Leonard—Camp Thomas Scott, Fort Wayne, Ind. | | 36 |
| Wilkes, Frederick—410 King, Athens, Ga. | | 63 |
| Wilkinson, Leo F.—Oxford, Ind. | | 48 |
| Williams, D. J.—5356 Lexington, Los Angeles, Calif. | | 93 |
| Williams, Frank R.—145 Johns, Marion, Ohio | | 24 |
| Williams, Leland B.—Monahans, Tex. | | 45 and 68 |
| Williams, Logen, E. | | 63 |
| Williams, Robert | | 12 |
| Williamson, Edward—Angola, Ind. | | 29 |
| Wilson, Bill—Crisfield, Md. | | 103 |
| Wilson, Wilfrod R.—Clearbrook, Va. | | 83 |
| Wingate, Richard D.—2483 Sylvan Village, Pontiac, Mich. | | 105 |
| Wise, Malcolm—Fairbanks, Alaska | | 33 |
| Wisner, Earl E.—Rt. 1, Antioch, Calif. | | 36 and 39 |
| Wisnoski, Arnold F.—11175 Findlay, Detroit, Mich. | | 29 |
| Witting, Edmond A.—Edgerton, Wis. | | 101 |
| Wokral, Earl J.—13413 Bartlett, Cleveland, Ohio | | 27 |
| Wolak, Joseph—992 E. Palmer, Detroit, Mich. | | 48 |
| Wolf, Walter S.—118 Whitfield, Boston, Mass. | | 91 |
| Wolfe, Judge E.—Box 72, Williams Fld., Chandler, Ariz. | | 25 and 101 |
| Wood, Harold L.—1301 W. Olympic, Los Angeles, Calif. | | 25 |

| NAME | ADDRESS | PAGE |
|---|---|---|
| Wood, John W.—409 S. Logan, Trenton, N. J. | | 33 |
| Wood, Leonard A.—232 Baden, Rochester, N. Y. | | 33 |
| Woodard, Ernest L.—4859 Kossuth, St. Louis, Mo. | | 95 |
| Woods, Joe D.—225 Carson, Pella, Iowa | | 102 |
| Wootton, Alfred A.—RFD 1, Box 118, Buckeye, Ariz. | | 48 and 93 |
| Worton, Robert A.—Somerset Centre, Mass. | | 32 |
| Wright, Brandon M.—West Tisbury, Marthas Vineyard, Mass. | | 95 |
| Wright, John R.—512 Riverside, Chino, Calif. | | 11 |
| Wright, Willard—McVeigh, Ky. | | 85 |
| Wunderlich, Bernard—105th Street, Brooklyn, N. Y. | | 35 |
| Wyley, Bernard J.—5010 W. Concord, Chicago, Ill. | | 31 |
| Wzykowski, Frank—48-29 209 Bayside, Long Island, N. Y. | | 60 |

### Y

| | | |
|---|---|---|
| Yaeger, Jack—711 7th, Tallahassee, Fla. | | 25 |
| Yellin, Jerome—160 Grumman, Newark, N. J. | | 31 |
| Yount, Barton K. | | 96 |
| Young, Dick—Fairbanks, Alaska | | 33 |
| Young, Jack M.—Helena, Ark. | | 11 |
| Young, Jessie—Elmara, Pa. | | 65 |
| Youngcross, Dominic—1117 Verona, Youngstown, Ohio | | 20 |

### Z

| | | |
|---|---|---|
| Zanes, Delaney C.—18 Tremont, Irvington, N. J. | | 60 |
| Zimmerman, Charles—Brooklyn, N. Y. | | 11 |
| Zimmerman, Harry C.—5339 Fortieth, Minneapolis, Minn. | | 91 |
| Zipin, Martin J.—2320 N. 29th, Philadelphia, Pa. | | 103 |
| Zuccarell, R. P.—5218 W. North Ave., Chicago, Ill. | | 61 |